microscope

a fractal role-playing game of epic histories, by Ben Robbins

Written by Ben Robbins

Edited by Ping Lin & Carole Robbins

Playtested for two years by 158 of the best gamers anyone could ask for.

Published by Lame Mage Productions

www.lamemage.com

First Edition 2011 (Print & PDF)

ISBN 978-0-9832779-0-3

Dedicated to my Father, Michael Robbins,
the very first person I told about Microscope.

Table of Contents

WHAT IS MICROSCOPE?
What You Need to Play 8
How To Use This Book 8

STARTING A NEW GAME
Step 1: Big Picture 10
    Quick Start History Seeds 11
Step 2: Bookend History 12
Step 3: Palette–Add or Ban Ingredients ... 13
Step 4: First Pass 15

PLAYING THE GAME
Overview of Play 18
Picking the Focus 19
Making History 20
Making History: Periods 22
Making History: Events 24
    You Build on Each Other... 27
    ... But Don't Collaborate 27
    Nuking Atlantis 28
Making History: Scenes 29
    Scene Step 1: State the Question 30
    Scene Step 2: Set the Stage 30
    Scene Step 3: Choose Characters 31
    Scene Step 4: Reveal Thoughts 32
    Option: Staying in the Background 33
    Option: Playing Time as a Character ... 33
    Is That Light or Dark? 37
Playing Scenes 38
    Answering the Question 38
    You Can't Change the Future 38
    Shaping the World: What
        You See Is What You Get 39
    Speaking Truth & Hearsay 40
    Thinking Out Loud 40
    Playing Secondary Characters 41
    Doing Things To Characters 42
    Push: Creative Conflict 43
    Starting With a Push 45
    Push: Describing Things No One Can See ... 45
    Push: The "You Already Knew That" Clause ... 46
Dictating Scenes 50
Ending Scenes 51
Legacies 52
    Choose a New Legacy 52
    Explore a Legacy 52
    Style of Play: Getting in
        the Microscope Mindset 53
Ending the Game 56
    Storing Your History 56
    Continuing Your History 56

DISCUSSION & ADVICE
History Seeds 58
Teaching Microscope 59
    Teaching Step 1: Explain the Concept 59
    Teaching Step 2: Game Setup 59
    Teaching Step 3: Explain Play 60
    Teaching Step 4: Be the First Player 60
    Teaching Step 5: Playing the First Scene 61
    Teaching Step 6: Next Player 61
    Onward... 62
Play Advice 63
    What's a Good Idea for a History? 63
    Beware Time Travel & Immortality 64
    Choosing Your Bookend Periods 64
    Number of Players 64
    How Do I Make a Good Focus? 65
    How Do I Make a Good Question? 66
    Implied Incidents: Keeping
        Track of What's Not on the Table 68
    Incomplete Ideas: Blind Man's Bluff 69
    World-Building & Spawning a New Game 70

AFTERWORD
How Microscope Works 72
    Great Power Without Great Responsibility ... 72
    The Hotseat 73
    Independence & Interdependence 74
    Fruitful Mistakes 75
    Time Is Not So Confusing After All 76
Thanks 78
Playtesters 79
Reference Sheet 80

WHAT IS MICROSCOPE?

Microscope works differently than some other role-playing games you might have played, so let's abandon some preconceptions:

You won't have your own character.

You won't play the game in chronological order. You may know all about the future, but be surprised by the past.

You'll build the story from the outside in. You'll decide the big picture, the grand scheme of history, and then burrow down and carve out the details.

It's fractal gaming.

So think big: you have a massive chunk of history to play around in.

Humanity spreads to the stars and forges a galactic civilization…

Fledgling nations arise from the ruins of the empire…

An ancient line of dragon-kings dies out as magic fades from the realm…

These are all examples of Microscope games.

In Microscope, you build an epic history as you play. Want to play a game that spans the entire *Dune* series, the *Silmarillion,* or the rise and fall of Rome in an afternoon? That's Microscope.

But you don't play the history from start to finish, marching along in chronological order. Instead, you build your history from the outside in. You start off knowing the big picture, the grand scheme of what happens, then you dive in and explore what happened in between, the how and why that shaped events.

You are free to jump backwards or forwards, zooming in or out to look at whatever you want, defying limits of time and space. Want to leap a thousand years into the future and see how an institution shaped society? Want to jump back to the childhood of the king you just saw assassinated and find out what made him such a hated ruler? That's normal in Microscope.

You have vast creative authority. You can make whole empires rise and fall at will. Dream up a utopia or destroy one with nuclear fire. You have that power, but remember you're not alone: everyone else at the table can do it too.

You create independently, but not in isolation. Each facet you add to history builds on what other players built before you. You expand on their ideas, and they expand on yours. History might not turn out the way you expected. Be prepared to think on your feet.

When you zoom all the way in to a particular moment in time, all the players share the stage and role-play together to find out something we want to learn about the history. Did the crew of the Icarus know the aliens were on Titan? Did the rebels really fake the government crackdown? Do the knights remember the original meaning of their ritual vows? We role-play and see.

The more you play, the more your once simple summary becomes a detailed tapestry, full of meaning and surprises. History snowballs.

What You Need to Play

Microscope is for two to five players, but three or four are best. There's no game prep and no GM. You can play a single session, or keep coming back and exploring the same history over and over again.

You'll need a stack of index cards and something to write with, along with table space to lay everything out. Smaller cards, like blank flash cards, work even better because they take up less space on the table.

How To Use This Book

These rules are written as step-by-step instructions that you can read aloud as you go, but I recommend that at least one person reads the whole thing before you sit down and play. Seeing the big picture of how the game works will make it easier to understand how each piece of the puzzle fits.

It's written so that (ideally) when you're sitting at the table playing, knee-deep in your history, you can easily flip to any section, find the rule you're looking for quickly, and go straight back to playing. The rules are intentionally very terse, so you don't have to wade through blocks of text to find the important bits. Examples are indented and italicized, and secondary information or commentary is in grey boxes.

I saved the discussion of how and why Microscope works for the appendix. It's interesting stuff, the sum of what we learned from playing this unusual game for the last two years, but it's not something you need to know to get started playing.

If the rules seem dry or boring, that's because the interesting part, the creative spark of the game, is only going to happen when you sit down at the table and play…

STARTING A NEW GAME

History starts out as a fairly blank slate, just a broad outline of what happens, but as each player takes turns adding new elements, you'll see more and more detail emerge.

At the beginning you'll collaborate and bounce ideas off each other to make sure you are on the same page about the kind of game you want to play, but partway through the setup that stops. From then on, the game demands that each player contribute their own ideas about how the history should unfold.

Sometimes you'll make decisions without knowing exactly where the whole thing is going, or whether what you're creating will turn out to be important. That's okay. Part of the fun is not being in complete control and being surprised by the very history you're helping to create, rather than planning it all out as a group.

To start a new game, follow these steps:

1) Big Picture

2) Bookend History

3) Palette–Add or Ban Ingredients

4) First Pass

Step 1: Big Picture

First, brainstorm a simple overview of the history you want to play. If you were looking in a history book, this would be the one line that summarizes what happens, but leaves out all the details. It should be no more than a single sentence.

> *An ancient empire rises and falls.*

> *Cavemen at the dawn of time found the first civilization.*

> *Mankind leaves the sick Earth behind and spreads out to the stars.*

Pick something big. You want a lot of time and space to work with.

Don't worry if your idea seems too simple or uninteresting. That's normal at this stage. Fleshing out the interesting details is what the rest of the game is all about.

Quick Start History Seeds

Having trouble coming up with the big picture for your history? Just pick one of these three history seeds, answer the questions to customize it, and you're ready to go.

Answer the questions as minimally as possible: don't brainstorm more about the history, and don't start fleshing out details. That will come out during play.

"Three nations are united as a single empire"

- ◆ What kind of nations are they? Feudal kingdoms, primitive tribes, modern superpowers, stellar clusters, or colonies on an alien world?

- ◆ Do the people of these nations share the same culture? Are they even the same race?

"Refugees carve out a new life in a distant land"

- ◆ Where is the distant land? A continent across the sea, a planet circling a lonely star, or a hidden magical realm?

- ◆ What are they fleeing? Religious persecution, environmental collapse, zombie hordes, or the oppressive hand of a dark overlord?

"A new force changes society, wiping away the old values"

- ◆ What is the force? Technology, a spreading religion, emerging superheroes, thought-police?

- ◆ If it's technology, what kind? Steam, gunpowder, industrialization, nanotech, warp gates, Atlantean alchemy, or the alphabet?

After you've answered the questions, rephrase the summary to match and you've got the big picture of your history.

> *Religious refugees carve out a new life in the fertile land beyond the wastes.*

You can use these same starting points over and over again and wind up with a completely different history each time, but if you need more, there's a longer list of History Seeds later on.

Step 2: Bookend History

Your history will be divided into **Periods**. Each Period is a very large chunk of time, probably decades or centuries.

Describe how your history begins and ends. These are your starting and ending Periods, the bookends of your history. You'll add more Periods later on, but everything will be between these points.

1) Agree on a short description for each Period, just a few sentences or a paragraph at most, painting a clear picture of what happens during that time.

2) Decide whether each description is Light or Dark, whether what happens during that Period is generally happy or tragic. This is the **Tone** of each Period. The Tone of the starting and ending Period do not have to match.

You can describe either Period first, as you prefer. Sometimes it's easier to pick Light or Dark for each Period, then see what ideas emerge.

> *Our concept is "mankind leaves the sick Earth behind and spreads out into the stars." We decide to have a Light starting Period and a Dark ending Period.*
>
> *Start Period (Light): Earth is in sad shape, but mankind unites to face the challenge and make a new life among the stars. It's not easy, but it's a time of hope and unity.*
>
> *End Period (Dark): Humanity is scattered across a myriad of star systems with no central connection or core identity. Isolated and alone, humanity fades into stagnation.*

Write each Period on a card, with an empty or filled circle for Light or Dark respectively. Orient the card tall, not wide. You don't have to write the whole description, just a short note to define the Period. Write start and end at the bottom of the cards to show that these are the boundaries of your history. Put your starting Period on the left and the ending Period on the right.

We now know how the history begins and how it ends, but we have no idea what happens in between. Finding out what happens in the middle, how history got from point A to point B, is what we do in the rest of the game.

Step 3: Palette–Add or Ban Ingredients

Next you take a step back and create your history's **Palette**. The Palette is a list of things the players agree to reserve the right to include or, conversely, outright ban. It gets everyone on the same page about what belongs in the history and what doesn't.

Make two columns, one for Yes and one for No:

1) Each player can add one thing, either a Yes or No.

    Add something to the **Yes** column if you think the other players would not expect it to be in the history, but you want to be able to include it.

    Add something to the **No** column if you think the other players would expect it to be in the history, but you don't want it included.

    Players can go in any order. You don't have to add anything to the Palette if you don't want to.

2) If every player did add something (either a Yes or No), repeat step 1: each player has the option to go again. If someone opted not to add something, stop: your Palette is done. In the end, no player will have added two things more than anyone else.

Feel free to discuss and negotiate. No one should be unhappy about what winds up added or banned on the Palette.

♦   If something is in the Yes column, then during the rest of the game it's okay to introduce it into the history even if it doesn't seem like it fits. You've all agreed it belongs.

♦   If something is in the No column, it's never okay to bring into the game, no matter what. You've all agreed it's not part of the history.

Even if something is in the Yes column, it doesn't exist in the history until someone introduces it in play. Something might be in the Yes column, but never get used at all.

The Palette is not an exhaustive list of what will be in the history: it's a list of exceptions. If something fits the setting (like wizards in a fantasy world), you probably don't need to add it to the Yes column because the other players already expect it. Likewise if something seems really out of place (like wizards in a science fiction history), you probably do not need to add it to the No column unless you think other players want to include it. When in doubt, discuss.

> One players puts "habitable worlds" in the No column. People have to live in artificial habitats, biodomes, space stations, or ships. Another player asks if terraformed worlds would be okay, but the first player doesn't want that either. The other players decide to go along with it.

> Another player adds "aliens" to the Yes column; she's not sure the other players want aliens in this setting, so she wants to find out now. Other players want to keep space mysterious, so after some discussion a different player adds "communication with aliens" to the No column. There may turn out to be aliens in the game, but there will be no way to talk to them.

The Palette is your last chance to freely negotiate and build group consensus about your history. Your choices tell the other players what kind of game you want to play, helping you avoid bad surprises and misunderstandings later on. If there's a big disagreement about the kind of things you want in your history, now's the time to find out and talk about it.

Step 4: First Pass

Group decisions are now over. For the rest of the game, each player makes decisions individually and has vast power to shape history.

Each player now gets to add more detail to the history, creating either a new Period or Event. Players can go in any order they want.

- To add a **Period**, place it between any two adjacent Periods, then give a short description of what happens during that time. Say if the Tone is Light or Dark.

- An **Event** is a specific thing that happens inside a Period, like a prince seizing the throne or a colony ship arriving on a new world. To add a new Event, decide what Period the Event is in. If there are already other Events in that Period, place it before or after one of them. An Event must be inside an existing Period. Tell the other players what happens during the Event. Say if the Tone is Light or Dark.

Write each Period and Event on a separate index card as you create them. Orient Event cards wide instead of tall (so you can tell them apart from Periods) and place them below the Period they are in. Cards are laid out in chronological order, with time flowing to the right for Period cards, and downward for Event cards within each Period. So each Period happens sometime after the Period to its left, and each Event happens sometime after the Event above it in the same Period.

MANKIND MAKES
NEW LIFE AMONG
STARS

(START)

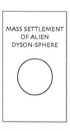

MASS SETTLEMENT
OF ALIEN
DYSON-SPHERE

"UNIFIERS"
CONQUER
MULTIPLE STAR
SYSTEMS

HUMANITY
STAGNATES
ISOLATED & ALONE

(END)

SURVEY SHIP "MEADOWLARK"
DISCOVERS SPHERE

SOLAR FLARES
DESTROY HUMAN SETTLEMENTS

What you write on the card is just a placeholder for the description you give the other players. What you say is more important than what is on the card. Always speak first, make sure the other players hear and understand you, then write.

Making Events and Periods is covered in more detail later on.

You now know a lot more about your history than you did when you started, and you're ready to start regular play.

PLAYING THE GAME

Overview of Play

You should have already followed the steps in "Starting a New Game" to build the foundation of your history.

Decide which player will start: that player becomes the first **Lens**. If someone is teaching the game, they should be the first Lens. You can give the Lens a large and visible object to remind everyone at the table who it is.

1) Declare the Focus: The Lens declares the current **Focus** of the game, the part of history you're going to explore right now.

2) Make History: Each player takes a turn creating either a Period, Event or Scene. The Lens goes first, then go around the table to the left. What you create *must* relate to the current Focus.

   The Lens can choose to create two things on her turn, so long as they are nested inside each other: either a new Event plus a Scene inside that Event, or a new Period plus an Event inside that Period. This gives the Lens more power to get the Focus going.

3) Lens Finishes the Focus: After each player has taken a turn, the Lens gets to go again and add another Period, Event or Scene (or two nested things). This lets the Lens have the last word about the Focus.

After all players have addressed the Focus, we take a step back and examine **Legacies**, elements of the history we want to remember to explore later on:

4) Choose a New Legacy: The player to the right of the Lens picks something from play during this last Focus and makes it a Legacy.

5) Explore a Legacy: The same player creates an Event or dictated Scene that relates to one of the Legacies, either the one just created or one already in play.

6) New Lens: The player to the left of the Lens then becomes the new Lens and picks a new Focus. Repeat.

Before the new Lens starts, you may want to take a quick intermission and talk about how the game is going. Talk about what you've liked or what intrigues you, but don't plan what's going to happen next.

That's the whole game in a nutshell. Each step is described in more detail in the rest of the book.

Picking the Focus

Play can jump backwards and forwards in time, all across the history. To keep everyone playing the same game, the Lens picks a Focus, a unifying theme that ties the story together, at least until the next Lens picks a new one.

The Focus can be anything: a person, a place, a thing, an institution, an Event, a Period, a concept–anything you want. The Lens can use something that already came up in play or make up something new on the spot. If you're making something new, you'll usually declare the Focus, then make a Period, Event or Scene to show what you're talking about.

> *"The new Focus is going to be the 'sinking of the Gabriel Dora.' It's a luxury liner that goes down mysteriously, so first I'm making a new Event where the ship sinks in the North Atlantic, with no known survivors…"*

Write down each Focus and who chose it on a card so that, as the history unfolds, you can look back and see how you explored it. If a new Lens is interested in a previous Focus, they could pick the same Focus again or pick a related Focus that looks at things from a different angle.

> *The old Focus was President Galveston, patriarch of the Lone Star Republic. During play we found out he died in office, eaten away by illness. The new Lens wants to explore that, so she makes the new Focus "the last days of Galveston's presidency."*

Picking the Focus is powerful. It lets you set the direction of the game. Don't hesitate to make up a Focus even if you don't have a clear idea why it's interesting. Those details will emerge as you play.

WHEN IN DOUBT

Pick a small, concrete Focus, like a particular person or an incident, rather than a broad or vague one. The narrower the Focus, the more detailed and personal the history will be to play.

Making History

On your turn, you can create either a **Period**, an **Event**, or a **Scene** (or two nested things if you're the Lens). These are the building blocks that outline your history: Periods show us the big picture, the broad sweep of history, Events zoom in closer and explore specific incidents within a Period, and Scenes zoom all the way in and reveal what happens moment-by-moment within an Event.

When you make a Period or an Event, you have vast power to shape history. You can add anything you want as part of your description, spontaneously creating–or destroying–people, places, or things.

> *A player adds a new Event "the King's army destroys the secret stronghold of the Moon Cultists, who are trying to unite the seven pieces of the sacred sword, Invictus." Neither the king, the cult or the sword had been mentioned before. The current player just made them all up.*

If you choose to play a Scene instead, you give up absolute control and invite the other players to role-play and decide what happens together.

No one owns anything in the history. It doesn't matter who created something: when it's your turn you can do anything you want with it. The only limits to your creativity are:

- Don't contradict what's already been said.

- Make sure what you add relates to the current Focus.

- Don't use anything from the No column of the Palette.

Only the current player gets to contribute. Other players should not give suggestions or ideas, and the current player cannot ask for input either. Other players can and should ask for clarification if they can't visualize what the current player is describing.

PERIOD CARD	**EVENT CARD**	**SCENE CARD**

20

You must show how what you are creating relates to the Focus. If it isn't clear, the other players should ask how it relates.

> *The Lens declared the Focus to be "the fall of the capitol city" during an ongoing war and made an Event for it. A player could add a Scene in that Event (a battle to hold the gate), create a separate Event (an army seeking vengeance against the invaders), or even make a distant Scene in a totally different Period (archaeologists sifting through the ruins of the city a thousand years later).*

Paint a clear picture. Particularly with Events, the other players should be able to visualize what physically happens. Other players don't get input, but they should ask questions if there's something they need to know to understand what you're creating.

> *"Tarsus colony is destroyed" is a good starting point for an Event, but it's too vague. If we were watching from a birds-eye view, we would probably see how the colony was destroyed. Did it blow up? Was it invaded? "A reactor accident destroys the Tarsus biodome" or "killer machines demolish the colony" paint a more complete picture.*

How much detail should you include? A good rule of thumb is to describe what would be visible from a birds-eye view at the level of history you're creating. If you're making a Period, your description should include the broad sweeps of history, but not specific details that would emerge during an Event or Scene. If you're making an Event, zoom in closer and describe what happens, but not the moment-by-moment detail of a Scene.

Remember to declare the outcome. There's a natural tendency to describe a starting situation, but not the conclusion. But in Microscope we already know how it ends. You always see the big picture before you zoom in and explore the details. Even if we never examine this part of history further, we should have a clear (but perhaps simplistic) sense of what happened.

> *"The President runs for re-election" is a bad Event, because it doesn't tell us the outcome. Does he win? Does he lose? The result is something we could easily see, so it should be part of the description. Without that information, the description is a cliffhanger, not a summary.*

There's always room between two items in the history. If you have two Periods, you can always add another Period in the middle, provided you describe it in a way that doesn't contradict what's already known.

Making History: Periods

A Period is the largest subdivision of the history. It is a very large chunk of time, usually decades or centuries depending on your history, like an era of feudal wars or stellar colonization.

To make a new Period:

1) Decide when it is: Place the new Period between any two adjacent Periods–the Period to the left is earlier, the one to the right is later.

2) Describe the Period: Give the other players a grand summary of what happens during this time or what things are like. Describe how it is different from other Periods around it, as appropriate.

3) Say whether it is Light or Dark: Explain how that Tone fits your description. You're never wrong about Tone, but you do have to justify your choice to the other players.

Write your Period description on an index card, oriented tall, with an empty or filled circle to show Light or Dark respectively. You don't have to write the whole description, just a short note to define the Period. Put your card where you indicated it goes in the history.

Your world can change drastically from Period to Period. Kingdoms can rise and fall, and whole technologies or schools of thought can be discovered or lost. Be sure to describe how the Period you are making is different from other Periods around it, as appropriate.

> *"This is before the colonies build the warp-net, but they have developed faster star drives, so you can travel between worlds in a few weeks rather than years. Interstellar commerce and travel is now commonplace. The New Sun faith from the 'Crusades' Period is everywhere, but it's not a fervent belief anymore, just customs and traditions everyone shares without thinking about it."*

Your description can include how the new Period relates to the Periods around it. But even if you visualize your Period as coming right before or after another Period, someone else could add a Period in between them later on, so long as their description of their Period doesn't contradict what was already said.

> *There's already a "the gods curse the world with endless winter" Period, and you make a new Period right before it: "A golden age of prosperity, the calm before the accursed winter." You visualize the golden age leading right up to the winter Period, but later another player adds a Period*

between them where the clans become proud and turn away from the sacred rituals, angering the gods. You didn't expect it, but it doesn't violate anything in the description of either Period, so it's okay.

Note that you don't specify exactly how long a Period is. Your description may include a broad sense of how much time is passing ("it's a war that rages for generations" or "this is decades after the revolution"), but we never count years or worry about exactly how long something is.

EXAMPLE: MAKING A PERIOD

On a player's turn, she says: "I'm making a new Period after the 'Peace of Ulrix' and before the 'Coming of the Western Kings.' It's a time of great terror, with evil wraith-spirits possessing and corrupting the lords of the realms, from the king on down. There's oppression and terrible deeds, and the people live in terror of their once-noble lords. The gleaming courts of chivalry become places of nightmare. And yes, it's Dark."

Another player asks for clarification about how that relates to something from earlier in the game: "Does that include the descendents of High King Ulrix? I assume they'd have the power to resist that kind of thing." The player making the Period won't say because she thinks that much detail wouldn't be visible at the Period level. To find out, someone will have to zoom in and make an Event in this Period.

After she's finished speaking, she writes 'Lords of Shadow, nobles possessed' on a card, draws a Dark circle, then places it in the history. Her turn is over.

LORDS OF
SHADOW,
NOBLES
POSSESSED

Making History: Events

An Event is something specific that happens during a Period, like a great battle or a festival. While a Period encompasses everything that happens across a large span of time, an Event describes what happens at a particular time and place. Just like Periods, the literal length of an Event is not important. Some Events may seem long, others very short.

To make a new Event:

1) Decide when it is: Place the Event in an existing Period. You cannot have an Event outside a Period. If there are already other Events in that Period, place it before or after one of them chronologically.

2) Describe the Event: Tell the other players what happens. Your description should be specific enough that the other players have a clear picture of what physically takes place. Make sure to include the outcome, not just the start.

3) Say whether it is Light or Dark: Explain how that Tone fits your description. You're never wrong about Tone, but you do have to justify your choice to the other players.

Write your Event description on an index card, oriented wide instead of tall, with an empty or filled circle to show Light or Dark respectively. You don't have to write the whole description, just enough to remind everyone what the Event is. Put your card where you indicated it goes in the history.

As play continues, each Event could wind up with multiple Scenes inside it, each one showing us more detail about what happened during that Event.

If you start to make an Event that describes something that is part of an existing Event, make a Scene inside of that Event instead. Anything that builds up to or describes the aftermath of what was described in an Event (like a meeting planning an upcoming attack, or the survivors escaping after that attack) is probably a Scene in that Event, not a separate Event. Avoiding split Events helps keeps your history manageable and easier to grasp: instead of having several Event cards that really just describe one thing, you'll have a single Event card summarizing the core concept, with all the related Scene cards tucked neatly beneath it.

> *There's already an Event, "The Owl guns down mob boss Segretti at his trial." A player wants to make an Event where the vigilante hero gets caught by police for the shooting, but the other players point out that if it happens soon after, not years later, it's really a Scene inside that same Event.*

EXAMPLE: MAKING AN EVENT

On the next player's turn, he says "I'll make an Event in this 'Lords of Shadow' Period. A warrior-prince who's a direct descendent of High King Ulrix sneaks into the castle of a shadow-tainted Duke to rescue his sister, who the Duke has captured and plans to wed. The prince and princess had both been in hiding, and they had escaped corruption. The Event is totally Dark."

He has described a situation, but not the outcome, so another player asks him to declare the visible outcome. "Oh, right. The prince tries valiantly, but he's discovered and slain. His sister does not escape. Hence the Dark."

He writes 'Prince, heir of Ulrix, slain trying to save sister from marriage to shadow Duke' on a card, draws a filled in circle for Dark, then puts the card beneath the 'Lords of Shadow' Period. His turn is done.

Later on, a different player decides to spend her turn exploring some of what led up to the princess's abduction. She says "I'm interested in this Duke who abducted the princess. I don't think he was always such a bad guy."

"I'm making an Event earlier in the Period, before this Duke was tainted by the wraith-spirits. He's much younger, and he's not the Duke yet. His father still rules. He's just a young noble knight. We didn't name him before, but I'm going to give one now. Let's call him Colliard."

"The Event is that the same princess from the other Event is sent to the Duke's domain for the summer to keep her safe from some potential danger at the court, and the

Duke makes his son her guardian and knight-protector. She's only a girl back then, but despite their age difference Colliard and the princess become fast friends. She even has a childish crush on her protector. It's Light, a pleasant summer of youth."

Another player asks "So wait, years earlier she's a welcome guest in the same castle she gets abducted to later on? By her childhood friend / guardian?"

"Yep, that's right."

"Dude. I can't decide if that's better or worse…"

As the other players mull the new light this casts on what they already know happens in the future, the current player writes 'Princess spends summer as ward of Duke, Colliard's father' on a card, draws an empty circle for Light, and puts it beneath the 'Lords of Shadow' Period, but above the 'Warrior-prince tries to free sister' Event. For good measure she also jots Duke Colliard's name on that Event card, so it's clear they're the same person. Her turn is done.

You Build on Each Other…

When you describe a Period, Event or the setup for a Scene, sell it. Pitch your vision to the other players. Paint a picture in vivid colors. Breathe life into it. Other players can't veto, but if they aren't interested or don't understand your idea, they won't build on it. In traditional game terms, for the moment you are the GM, making the other players believe in your world. Speak with authority, like you're describing a real thing you can see.

Microscope is all about building on each other's ideas. Every player has immense creative power and can invent whole chunks of history all by themselves, but they're also dependent on each other. Even if you're the Lens, you can't create a Scene along with an Event and Period to contain it all in one swoop. More likely you'll build an Event in a Period someone else made, or a Scene in someone else's Event. To make what you want, you have to listen to what other people have made and think of how to expand on it.

Sometimes it works the other way: you'll create something you think is dull or obvious, but it inspires another player to build on it in a way you didn't foresee. Your "boring" idea can snowball into something unexpected and wonderful. So don't be afraid to create something simple: you may be providing a valuable foundation for someone else.

… But Don't Collaborate

Nothing will kill your game faster than playing by committee. When it's someone else's turn, don't coach. Explaining the rules is fine, but don't suggest ideas. Even if another player wants ideas, don't give them. Let them come up with something.

Be interested in what other players create. Ask questions, demand clarification. If there are contradictions, point them out, but resist the urge to make suggestions, even tiny ones. You've already inspired them with your contributions to the history. Now wait and see what they do with it. Keep your poker face.

If you collaborate and discuss ideas as a group, you'll get a very smooth and very boring history. But if you wait and let people come up with their own ideas, they may take the history in surprising and fascinating directions. It can be hard to sit silently and watch someone think, but the results can be awesome. You'll get a chance to interact more fluidly when you role-play Scenes.

Nuking Atlantis

Or "Can I just say that guy is dead?"

It doesn't matter who created that gleaming city on the hill or who played that character in the last Scene: if it's your turn, you can do whatever you want. No one owns anything in the history. You can make an Event and say "this is when the Prophet gets assassinated" or "this is when that awesome city you guys have been going on about gets nuked. Boom!" You have nigh unlimited power, so long as you don't contradict what's already been established.

Don't pull your punches. Killing a character or nuking a city doesn't remove it from the game because you can always go back in time and explore what it was like when it was still around. No matter what you do, other players can still go back and use it, so don't be afraid to wipe things out. Nothing is ever removed from the history. The past is never closed.

Making History: Scenes

Scenes are the smallest units of history. They show us exactly what happens at a specific place, at a specific time, with specific people. Scenes are also different because, instead of creating them unilaterally, all the players join in and role-play to determine what happens. You give up absolute control, but in return you get to decide what everyone is going to role-play about, turning everyone's attention to a part of the history that interests you.

To create a Scene, you first pose a Question, something you want to find out about the history. The goal of the Scene is to decide the answer to that Question. We start off the Scene without an answer and discover it through play. The Question can tell us something crucial to history ("why did the king betray his country?"), it can give us a window into what life was like in that time and place ("are the asteroid miners happy with their rugged frontier lives?"), or just examine something that isn't important in the grand scheme of things, but is interesting to the players ("did the soldier get to marry his hometown sweetheart?").

If you want to make a Scene, but you want to answer the Question yourself instead of letting the other players participate, you can choose to **dictate** the Scene instead. When you dictate a Scene, you describe what happens and narrate the answer to your own Question, just like making a Period or Event. Making dictated Scenes is covered later.

To make a played Scene, don't say anything about what you have in mind, just follow these steps:

1) State the Question

2) Set the Stage

3) Choose Characters (↺)

4) Reveal Thoughts (↺)

The ↺ symbol indicates choices made by each player, going around the table to the right (the opposite direction of normal play). All other decisions are made by the player making the Scene.

Scene Step 1: State the Question

State the Question this Scene will answer. The Question is why we are looking at the Scene in the first place, and the Scene isn't complete until we find the answer. A Question can be a simple yes/no or it can require a more detailed answer.

> *Are the rebels driven by vengeance or a desire for freedom?*
> *Can the World-AI recreate the long-dead human race?*
> *What do all mages have to sacrifice to learn sorcery?*
> *What's the one thing that can harm the god of beauty?*

A Question can establish facts or stack the deck. If something is declared in the Question, it's going to happen. There's no avoiding it. Craft your Question carefully to push the Scene in the direction you want to explore.

> *If the Question is "why does the king betray his country?",*
> *we know the king is going to do it. Nothing can prevent it.*
> *You would get totally different Scenes if you asked "Does*
> *the king betray his country?" or "What did the warlord pay*
> *the king to betray his country?"*

Write your Question in the top third of an index card, oriented tall (opposite of the way you write Events, so you can tell them apart). Keep the card out so everyone can look at the Question while playing the Scene.

Scene Step 2: Set the Stage

When does the Scene happen?: Decide which Event the Scene is in. If there are already Scenes in that Event, put it before or after one.

Review established facts: Refresh everyone's memory about things we already know that bear on this Scene. Don't create anything new at this point, just review what already happened and what we know is going to happen in the future. Other players can help out if they think of things.

> *"He hasn't done it yet, but we know from the description*
> *of the Event that the hero is going to win the Sword of*
> *Storms and defeat the Colossus."*

Where? Why? What Just Happened or What's Next?: Describe where the Scene physically takes place and what is going on. Are the characters here for a reason? Is there something they intend to do? What happened just before the Scene? If there are specific incidents implied in the Event description or the Question, say whether this is before or after.

> *"It's night-shift on the bridge of the Icarus, and the captain*
> *should be asleep but he's checking on his green crew. We*
> *know the ship is going to discover the ghost planet, but*
> *that hasn't happened yet. It's a normal cruise so far."*

Scene Step 3: Choose Characters

<u>Require and ban characters</u>: Player making the Scene may specify one or two characters someone must play in this Scene. That player can also name one or two characters no one can play in this Scene. These can be characters already introduced, or just descriptions of roles or relationships ("the doctor's son"). Banning seemingly essential characters can lead to very different Scenes.

You can require or ban categories of people (like police, nobles, or children), instead of specific individuals. You cannot ban groups by what they are not (such as banning anyone who is *not* a soldier), since that would create a requirement for all characters.

> *"I require the king and a secret heretic, and I ban the king's son and anyone from the neighboring kingdom."*

<u>Pick characters</u>: (all players ↺) Each player picks a character to play in the Scene. The person to the right of the player making the Scene picks first, then continue around to the right (opposite the direction of normal play). The player making the scene picks last. All required characters must be played, so if you're one of the last two players to pick you may be forced to choose a required character if they haven't already been taken.

You can invent a completely new person on the spot, or pick someone who has already appeared in the game, even if it's a character someone else played previously. All you need is a few words to describe the character, including any relationships they have to other characters.

> *A down-and-out miner, the king's lover, the lieutenant to the commander of the invasion force: each of those is all the detail you need to create a character.*

Your goal is to answer the Question, so pick a character that helps you do that. With some Questions certain characters may have a lot more power to decide the answer than others. Even if you can't pick a character who decides the answer, your choice may tell the other players where you want the Scene to go.

> *If the Question is "why does the gunslinger refuse to draw?" and you choose to play the gunslinger, the answer hinges on your decision. You're in control. Or you could choose a character that adds new details to influence the answer, like "the gunslinger's kidnapped girlfriend" or "his pacifist father." Is the gunslinger being blackmailed with the life of his girl? Did his father tell him to hang up his gun? We haven't even started the Scene yet, but the pot's brewing. There could be a lot of possible reasons, but in the end it's up to the person playing the gunslinger to show us what really made him refuse.*

31

Scene Step 4: Reveal Thoughts

Each player states one thing their character is thinking about the upcoming Scene. Start to the right of the player making the Scene and continue to the right (all players ↻, the same order as picking characters).

Your thought could reveal what your character is going to do or highlight what your character expects to happen. Revealed thoughts are a powerful tool for influencing the Scene. They let you give the other players hints about where you want the Scene to go.

Don't reveal thoughts that answer the Question before the Scene even starts–you can hint or stack the deck, but don't give a definite answer.

> *"The navigator wonders why they're really being sent to Korvis IV. He can't believe they'd send a ship all the way out here just to take spectrographic readings."*

Your thoughts can be about other players' characters, but you're only saying what your character thinks or believes. The other player gets to say what their character really did or is doing.

> *"The navigator thinks the Lieutenant sold them out to the Hegemony." Did the Lieutenant do it, or is the navigator barking up the wrong tree? The Lieutenant's player gets to decide. We'll see in play, or maybe when the Lieutenant reveals his thoughts.*

You're now ready to play the Scene. The player making the Scene can choose to say who is present when the Scene starts. Players can have other characters enter the Scene whenever they want.

Option: Staying in the Background

Some Scenes are better with fewer characters. The player making the Scene cannot require fewer characters, but any player can choose to play someone they consider a minor character and just stay in the background during the Scene, leaving the critical interactions to the important characters. Make sure to tell the other players that's your intention.

Option: Playing Time as a Character

Instead of playing a normal character, one player in a Scene can choose to play **Time**, a special type of character. Time represents forces or groups of people who are pushing the situation to some conclusion, for good or ill. The barbarians at the gates, the cavalry come to the rescue, the angry mob, the black plague, the tanking economy–these could all be Time.

> *A player decides to play the court nobility as Time. They are eager for the king to make a decision. If he doesn't stop waffling, they may take matters into their own hands.*

Time can be a required character, but the current player must define Time as something specific (angry senators, the barbarians, etc.) instead of just requiring "Time." When Time reveals thoughts, it should always be about how or why it wants to hurry things along.

Time makes more sense in some Scenes than others. One of Time's jobs is to put pressure on the Scene. If the Scene is going slow, it is up to Time to step in and push for a resolution, which may force the other players to hurry up and answer the Question. It's a little like being a GM in a traditional game: you can nudge the other players if they aren't getting anywhere, but if they are rolling, you should sit back and let things unfold. Playing Time is also useful when there are a lot of players at the table and more characters within the Scene would not improve anything.

EXAMPLE: MAKING A PLAYED SCENE

There are four players: Addie, Bors, Cat, and Dennis. They're conveniently sitting in alphabetical order clockwise around the table, just like the normal order of play (A-B-C-D).

They're playing a history where martial arts legends have passed down their teachings from generation to generation. Bors just went, so this is Cat's turn. She says "Let's play a Scene. The Question is 'why is the Master hesitant to trust this particular monk to save the secrets of the temple?' This is in the Event 'Temple on Seven Eagle Mountain destroyed by Emperor's troops' during the 'Emperors oppress the people' Period. I'm going to put it before the Scene where the Imperial general ordered his men to take no prisoners."

(established facts) "We already know the temple is going to be destroyed, but we saw in the 'War of Quiet Rivers' Period that the Seven Eagle martial arts style survived, even though it was thought lost for generations."

(what, where, why) "The Scene is taking place in one of the high-walled practice courtyards of the temple. The Master has kept the apprentice monk 'after class' and is putting him through grueling exercises, apparently in punishment for some failing. It's midday and the sun is beating down mercilessly, but in the background the snowy peak of the mountain seems to float, serene and cool."

"Oh, and we know the attack is going to happen later in the Event, but this is before the monastery has been alerted to the approaching soldiers. There's tension because of the trouble across the land, but otherwise it's just another day in the temple as far as most people are concerned, but the Masters can see the writing on the wall. They've discussed sending away promising disciples to ensure their school survives, but haven't told any of the students yet."

(banned & required) "For characters, I'm requiring the monk and his Master from the Question. They're the characters from the Scene description, in case that wasn't obvious. Hmm, I was going to ban the Emperor's soldiers but I don't think I will. I am going to ban the monk's brother, which implies that, yeah, he has a brother, but his brother can't be in this Scene. Not sure if that will have an impact, but it seems interesting. Time to pick characters."

Scene choices go in the opposite direction of normal play, so Bors goes first because it was his turn last. Cat will go after everyone else because she's making the Scene.

Bors: "I'll be the Master. It seems like he's got final word over the Question. He's relatively young, probably in his fifties."

Addie: "I'll play the monk's good-for-nothing best friend. He washed out of training, so now he's a menial servant / laborer in the temple." *She picked this character to raise doubts about whether the monk is a good student.*

Dennis: "I'll be the apprentice monk."

Cat: "All the required characters have been taken already, so I'll be another Master at the temple. I'm the ancient, blind, wise-but-enigmatic-parable guy, tottering along with my walking stick."

Bors asks Dennis to name the monk since he's going to be coming up a lot. Dennis asks for help, so they kick around ideas and decide to call him Wen.

Players reveal thoughts in the same order they picked characters.

Bors: "Wen's teacher is not sure Wen is disciplined enough. His head always seems to be in the clouds." *The other players ask whether he just answered the Question, which is forbidden before play starts.* "Hmm, maybe. Okay, scratch that. The Master is afraid for the school because he knows in his heart that only the strong survive in this world."

Addie: "The good-for-nothing best friend thinks Wen is wasting his time tricking his teachers into thinking he's so diligent. He'd be better off just taking it easy like me." *This is what the friend thinks, but it doesn't mean it's what Wen is really doing.*

Dennis: "Okay, Wen is secretly ashamed that he's broken his vow of chastity. Zinger!"

Cat: "Yow! Nice one. That gives me a lot of ideas, but I think I'll stick with being the straight man for now. The blind master wonders why Wen's teacher delays sending him into the wilds. The choice has been made. It's time to act. He fears time is running out. Now let's play."

35

Cat writes the Question on the top of the card, oriented tall, then writes the setting in the middle. For now they keep the card out where everyone can see the Question, but when the Scene is done, she'll write the answer on the bottom, draw a circle for Light or Dark, and then put it underneath the Event card, on top of the Scene that comes after it.

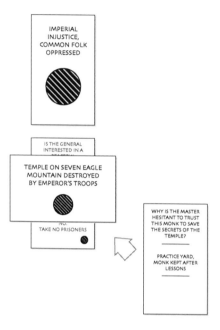

Is That Light or Dark?

Here's a secret: Light or Dark are entirely subjective. They depend on who you're rooting for.

Raiders sack a thriving port city. Do you think the people in the city are basically good people? If so, then you probably would think it was Dark that they were wiped them out. But what if those same citizens were despicable tyrants, oppressing their neighbors with fear and military might? Now those raiders look more like the purging hand of justice, come to wipe out evil and bring justice, and you might consider it Light.

There is no right or wrong answer. The important thing is to explain to the other players *why* you think something is Light or Dark.

When you're making history, you've already described what physically happens, what we would see if we watched history from the birds-eye view ("raiders sack the city," "the President calls for reform"). When you're picking Tone, you're deciding what you think it *means*. You're judging the history, applying your own sense of right and wrong, and explaining your thinking to the other players.

When you're judging Tone at the end of a Scene, it's a rare chance for the whole table to freely discuss what just happened and what you think it means. You'll disagree. You'll go back and forth. You'll think it's Dark, but then someone else will make an argument that makes you change your mind. That's good. You're establishing a shared sense of what it all means, what the point of this whole history is.

WHEN IN DOUBT:
Go with your gut. You're never wrong about Tone, so long as you can explain your choice. If you're judging a Scene and it doesn't seem strongly Light or Dark, make it the opposite Tone of the Event it's in.

Playing Scenes

Each player controls a character in the Scene and uses that character to try to answer the Question. There is no GM. During a Scene, you can:

- Role-play what your character does and thinks. If someone tries to do something to your character, you describe the outcome.

- Shape the world by describing what your character perceives and how they react to it.

- Introduce and play secondary characters, as needed.

During the Scene, **everyone should be trying to answer the Question**. Keep looking at the Question as you play. The Scene ends when the players know the answer to the Question. After the Scene is over, you will look at what happened and decide whether it was Light or Dark.

If another player makes something happen in the world outside their character, but you have a different idea of where the Scene should go or how the world should be, you can **Push** to change it: you suggest an alternative, and all the players vote to decide which one happens.

Those are all the rules for playing a Scene. Each part is described in more detail below.

Answering the Question

The Scene ends when the players know the answer to the Question. It doesn't matter if the characters know the answer or not. If you think the Question has been answered, just say "Hey, I think that answered the Question." If the other players agree, you're done with the Scene.

A player may answer the Question by having a character perceive something, do something, say something, or even just think something–it all depends what the Question was. Do you have an answer to the Question, but can't think of how to make your character blurt it out? Just say what your character is thinking instead. An internal monologue that reveals the answer to the players is good enough.

You Can't Change the Future

Playing Microscope is different than many games because we often know what is going to happen in the future: we know the kingdom is going to lose the war, we know the colony is going to be overrun. The Question may even declare that certain things are going to happen. The action within a Scene cannot change the facts that have been established, but they can change our assumptions about how or why things happened. Seeing exactly how things happened is the interesting part of the story.

Shaping the World: What You See Is What You Get

If you want to describe something about the world outside your character during the Scene, just describe your character perceiving it. You can make up anything you want this way, so long as it obeys the usual rules for making history (don't contradict what we already know, don't use anything banned by the Palette). You can make new things happen or reveal facts about the environment or world.

You want an alien fleet to appear, so you describe your character watching a sensor array and seeing the blips appear as they warp in. It's an alien fleet!

You want the President (a character no one is playing) to be an android, so right after another player shoots him you describe examining the body and seeing sparking circuits and wires in the wound. Boom, he's an android.

You must also describe your character reacting to what he or she perceives. You're role-playing in the moment, not just narrating a story.

"My secret service agent looks up from the President's android body, and he can't believe his eyes. He says: 'I don't understand… How can this be possible?!?'"

Don't describe things you perceive about a character someone else is playing, unless it's a secondary character (someone introduced during the Scene, not picked during setup). That's for the other player to decide.

When someone describes something they see, don't ignore it. Work with it. Build on what other people add during the Scene. Another option is to intentionally introduce something incomplete and then **pass the ball** to another player and let them fill in the details.

You describe your character noticing strange runes on the floor of the tomb, then ask another player "Doc, do you think that writing explains what happened here? I can't make heads or tails of it. Can you read it?"

PLAY

SCENES

Speaking Truth & Hearsay

Sometimes you'll just have your character say things about the world to establish that they're true. Generally this isn't any different than describing what you perceive: you're just describing something that your character knows because they perceived it in the past.

> *The soldier says "No one is coming to save you. The 7th Legion was slaughtered in the passes. We're on our own.' He looks out over the parapet, grimly ready for the final battle."*

Sometimes the opposite is true: you're not trying to establish a fact, you're just having your character express an opinion. You may even expect your character to turn out to be totally wrong. A character can be extremely confident but still be incorrect, because they're basing their beliefs on rumors, hearsay, or bad information. It's critical to communicate to the other players whether you are establishing facts or just expressing your character's opinion.

If you can't explain how your character perceived what you're describing, you can't establish it as true. It can only be opinion.

> *"My soldier character says 'There is no way the Corsairs can break the blockade. By the time our message reaches them, it will be too late.' But I'm not saying that's fact. That's just the soldier's glum opinion. He could be wrong."*

> *"The aliens are friendly, I tell you! They're thousands of years beyond our understanding!" But the Scene is set before anyone has made contact, so despite good intentions, the scientist's player has no way of showing how the character could know what the aliens are actually like. It must be opinion, not fact. In the long run, it may turn out to be true, or it may not.*

Thinking Out Loud

If you want to establish something but don't want your character to say it, just say what they're thinking. Maybe it wouldn't make sense for the character to blurt something out, or you just can't think of why they would bring it up right now. Just like Revealing Thoughts during Scene setup, describing a character's thoughts during play is a great way to show other players where you want to go in the Scene–even if you're hiding it from the characters. Telling the other players what you want in the Scene lets them help you get there. Characters can come and go quickly, so don't be shy about broadcasting their agendas.

"Trooper Cobb yells 'We can't leave Lansky behind! I don't care if none of you come. I'll do it alone!' But he's really just bluffing. He's being gung-ho to cover for the fact that this screw up was his fault in the first place."

Playing Secondary Characters

Each player has a main character they chose during Scene setup, but any player can also introduce and play secondary characters, as needed. Secondary characters might be people from previous Scenes or Events, or they might be characters made up on the spot. They can be used to bring background action to life or explore role-playing opportunities you didn't foresee during Scene setup. A secondary character isn't necessarily less important in the world; they're just someone who wasn't picked at the beginning of the Scene.

"You said your son's one of the other warrior-knights, right? Well, I think now's a good time for the hostages to be brought out. Hey, guess who?"

You can never introduce secondary characters banned during Scene setup.

You play the secondary character in addition to your main character for the rest of the Scene, or until you decide to hand the secondary character off to someone else. Avoid talking to yourself: if your main character is interacting meaningfully with a secondary character you control, give the secondary character to someone else to play.

Unlike a main character, another player can Push to change anything about a secondary character, including what they do or think. You don't have the same unique authority over a secondary character as you do over your main character.

If you want to describe someone unimportant doing something and you don't have any reason to keep role-playing that character, it's often easier to just describe the action as something your character perceives, rather than introducing a secondary character.

I want peasants to throw rocks at the witch as she's led to the stake. I could introduce a peasant as a secondary character, but instead I just say "My merchant watches as peasants pick up rocks and hurl them at the condemned witch. He's disgusted, but he knows the Faith demands it." Done.

Doing Things To Characters

Each player controls the fate of the character they chose during Scene setup. If you want to do something to someone else's character, describe what you are trying to do and your intended effect. It's up to the other player to decide the result.

> *A player says the gladiator character he controls tries to stab the Emperor and kill him. The Emperor's player gets to say if the Emperor is slain, wounded, or escapes the attack entirely.*

If you do something to a secondary character (anyone not picked during Scene setup), you get to declare the outcome, no matter who is playing the secondary character. That's true even if you are controlling a secondary character and having them do something to another secondary character: the actor decides the result.

> *The Emperor is protected by a pair of Praetorian guards, secondary characters introduced during the Scene. The player controlling the gladiator describes his character springing on the unwary soldiers and killing them before they can react. They're secondary characters, so it doesn't matter that another player controls them: the gladiator's player gets to decide what happens.*

Sometimes it's the other way around: you want another character to do something to your character. If no one is playing that character or it's a secondary character you control, just describe perceiving it and it happens. If it's a character someone else is playing, you can tell the other player what you want the character to do, but it's up to them to decide if they want to go along with it. If it's a secondary character someone else controls, you can Push for them to do something.

> *The player controlling the Emperor says that rioting peasants surge into the throne room and cut him down. The Emperor dies cursing the fickle masses.*

Push: Creative Conflict

If, while playing a Scene, someone describes something about the world outside their character and you have a different idea you like better, you can Push to substitute your idea for theirs. You are potentially winding back the clock and replacing what the other player said.

> *A player describes their astronaut character sweeping his flashlight across the interior of the drifting space hulk and seeing smashed consoles and wreckage. You propose that instead the ship is in perfect condition, and the crew are still standing at their posts, frozen in time…*

You may or may not get what you want. After the other players hear your idea, they may put forward proposals of their own. Once all the options are on the table, everyone votes to decide which one actually happens.

- ◆ When a player shapes the world by describing their character perceiving something, you can substitute what you describe instead. The character's reaction is still up to the other player.

- ◆ You cannot change someone else's main character, including what they do or think. The exception is that you can change what happens to them (such as Pushing that a character dodges a bullet rather than getting hit).

- ◆ You can change anything about secondary characters someone else controls: what they do or think, facts or details about them, or what happens to them.

You can only Push to change something someone just said. You can't go back and alter something from earlier in the Scene. You can only make changes while playing Scenes (not during Scene setup and not during dictated Scenes).

To Push your alternative, follow these steps:

1) Proposal: State your alternative simply and concisely (summarize, don't play it out). Be clear what you want to replace. Don't negotiate or discuss. Other players can ask for clarification if they're confused, but they cannot add or change details.

2) Additional Proposals: There are now two ideas: what the original player described during play, and the alternative put forward by a second player. The remaining players can propose their own alternatives, if they want. Each player states his or her idea, one at a time, in any order. Again, keep it concise, and don't negotiate or discuss.

All proposals must be alternatives to the original idea, not something unrelated. You can propose something that's a variation or refinement of someone else's proposal, so long as there is a meaningful difference.

No one can retract or change their proposal once it has been stated, including the original idea from play. Even if you like another idea more than the one you proposed, someone else may like your idea and want to vote for it. There can be as many proposals as there are players.

3) <u>Vote</u>: All players vote to decide which idea happens. Everybody votes simultaneously without discussion. Point one hand towards the person who proposed the idea you prefer (including yourself). Point from one to five fingers–the more fingers you point the more you want that thing to happen.

You can vote for two different proposals. Use a different hand for each. You can't use both hands for one. If you support all ideas equally, just hold up the Fist of Solidarity (aka the Rock or "those ideas all rock"). The rock is always positive because if you hated the ideas you would have proposed something different.

4) <u>Determine the winner</u>: Count fingers. Highest number wins. That proposal happens, the others don't. If there's a tie, the player who went first during Scene setup wins.

5) <u>Play the results</u>: The winner of the vote decides how to play out the result. You can *Narrate*, taking over the Scene temporarily and describing how what you proposed happens or is seen, or you can *Play* and let everyone role-play normally with the understanding that the winning proposal must occur and the players will work together to make it happen.

If the vote decided what a main character perceived, that player's character describes how they react. You can't Push to describe someone else's reaction.

After the Proposal is resolved, continue playing the Scene unless the Question has been answered. You can Push multiple times within a single Scene.

Starting With a Push

You don't have to wait for someone else to create something to Push your own idea. You can start a Push to describe something someone else's character perceives (but not their reaction) or to describe anything about a secondary character someone else controls.

> *A player describes his character getting ready for bed. You Push and say you want the character to find a bloody knife on the floor. Another player could counter propose the character seeing something different or there not being anything unusual at all. If you win the vote, then the knife is there and the character sees it, but the character's player gets to describe how they react.*

You have to declare that you're Pushing, so the other players know that they can suggest their own alternatives if they want. Follow the same procedure for an initial proposal: describe it succinctly, and don't discuss or negotiate.

If there are no counter proposals, you don't even need to vote: you win automatically.

Push: Describing Things No One Can See

In some cases, you may want to describe something without having any character perceive it (at least not yet). You must Push to do it, and you can only describe things that are relevant to the current Scene.

> *"Just after everyone falls into cryo-sleep, an indicator light on the control panel starts winking. It's a sensor alert showing that some foreign organism is aboard the ship. It's something no one can perceive, so I have to Push to make it happen. Anyone have a counter proposal?"*

Establishing something unseen doesn't mean a character can't perceive it later on. Any player could describe their character perceiving it. If you wanted it to remain unseen, you could Push to describe their character not perceiving it.

If you want to describe a person or creature taking action, just introduce that secondary character and describe what they're doing, as normal. You don't need to Push.

> *"I'm introducing a new secondary character. There's a ninja assassin hidden in the trees outside the temple. She's drawing back her bow, trying to identify her target from a mob of identically robed monks, but she can't spot him. She is determined to complete her mission at all costs."*

Push: The "You Already Knew That" Clause

During a Scene, you may want to describe something that retroactively changes what another player's character knows. Effectively, you are saying to the other player "you didn't know this until just now, but your character knew this all along."

This is a special case because you are changing the meaning of the role-playing that already happened in this Scene, recasting what was said and done in a potentially very different light. You may be completely altering the motivations of the characters. It can be confusing and disruptive for the other players.

The rule is: if you want to describe something that another player's character would already know, but it's news to the player, you must declare that's what you're doing and Push to make it true, even if it's something that would normally be within your power to describe. You are required to make it clear that this is what's happening, and the other players get to decide if they're okay with it.

> Your character is talking with the Captain about the mission, and you want to say that, before the Scene started, the ship got a distress signal, and that's why it landed on this asteroid. That's news to the other players, but their characters would already know it–they received the distress signal and chose to land their ship. You have to declare this is something "the characters already would have known" and Push to make it true.

> On the other hand, if you said there was a secret mission that only your character knew about, you would not be required to Push at all, because you're only establishing things about your own character.

You only need to invoke this rule when someone describes something that meaningfully changes what we thought the characters knew. Trivial changes, or facts that don't have an impact on current play, don't count.

It's the responsibility of the player making the change to declare that they are revising what the players knew and Push, but other players can and should point it out if that player doesn't.

EXAMPLE: PLAYING A SCENE AND PUSHING

It's a later Scene during the "destruction of the Temple on Seven Eagle Mountain" Event. The Question is "does Wen obey his Master and flee, or does he refuse to abandon his comrades?" Imperial soldiers have broken down the gates and are putting the monks to the sword. This time Addie is playing the Master and Cat is playing Wen. Bors is playing Time in the form of the encroaching soldiers and Dennis (who made the Scene) is playing another apprentice who's supposed to lead Wen off the mountain. They've been role-playing and the Master has just sent a reluctant Wen down a hidden tunnel out of the temple while he stays behind to hold off the soldiers, but Wen is dithering.

Dennis (guide monk): "The other apprentice monk is terrified. 'You heard the Master! If we do not flee now we suffer the same fate as the rest!'"

Cat (Wen): "Wen is torn: 'We can't just leave them! We have to help!' But he can't decide, so the Question isn't answered yet. He's not sure that even if he did stay he'd be strong enough to do any good. Poor Wen."

Bors (Soldiers as Time):"All very touching, but meanwhile the soldiers are storming through the temple, putting it to torch. Their excited yells draw closer to where the monks are hiding, so they'll be discovered soon..."

Addie (Master): "Not so fast! The lone Master steps out, blocking the soldiers from going farther. With fierce concentration he stretches his arms into the Seven Eagle Mountain stance. He knows he can't defeat the whole army, but they are going to rue the day they stepped into his temple! Rue the day! Whoop-ass unleashed! Soldiers go flying!"

Dennis (guide monk): "Remember, the soldiers as Time are Bors' main character, not secondary characters, so you state intent and he states results."

Addie (Master): "Oh right. The Master attacks the soldiers, with the intent to kick them out of the temple."

Bors (Soldiers as Time): "I think that's awesome and I'm fine with it, for now. The soldiers have been driving lowly monks like sheep, but now that they're up

*against a kung fu master, the shoe's on the other foot
and they crumble."*

*Dennis (guide monk): "The other monk is peering back
around the corner and sees this whirlwind of fists
and feet. He brightens and grabs Wen. 'See, they are
no match for our Master! He'll kick them right off the
mountain!'"*

Addie (Master): "Hell yeah!"

*Dennis (guide monk): "But then he sees a tall figure
wearing the robes of a Yellow Snake adept making
his way through the soldiers. He's coming forward to
face the Master. The apprentice is terrified because
Yellow Snake is a powerful kung fu school and the
Master could have met his match."*

*Bors (Soldiers as Time): "Wait, are you saying a martial
arts school is serving the Emperor?"*

*Dennis (guide monk): "My guy has no way to know, so I
can't establish it, but it sure looks that way."*

*Bors (Soldiers as Time): "I want to Push. My counter
proposal is that the figure is using the fighting style
of a Yellow Snake disciple, but he is wearing fancy
court garb instead of the traditional robes of his
order, so he's probably an outcast or renegade in the
pay of the Emperor."*

*Addie (Master): "So you're saying the Yellow Snake order
isn't associated with the Emperor?"*

*Bors (Soldiers as Time): "Well, I can't say they aren't, but
nothing here would indicate they are, if that makes
sense. That's me and Dennis: any other proposals?"*

*No one else has a proposal, so everybody votes. Bors wins.
It was Dennis' character whose perception was changed
by the Push (even though other characters can perceive
this as well), so he describes his revised reaction.*

*Dennis (guide monk): "Hmm, the apprentice is thinking
he's a renegade and, if anything, that makes him even
more worried for his Master because a despicable
outcast wouldn't be bound by any code of his order."*

*Addie (Master): "Ha! Bring it on yellow-belly! I mean, the
Master sees him and prepares for battle."*

Bors (Soldiers as Time): "Hey, can I play the renegade as a secondary character? You made him up Dennis, so if you'd rather I'd give you first dibs."

Dennis (guide monk): "That's cool, go ahead."

Bors (Soldiers as Time): "The Yellow Snake renegade sneers confidently. 'At last, a monk who chooses to fight rather than run away. So much the better. The Emperor's gold will not be nearly so great a reward as this chance to show how weak Seven Eagle Mountain style really is!'"

Addie (Master): "Oh, you're getting whoop-ass for that! Hey, you're a secondary character, so I get to describe the outcome! The Master crushes the Yellow Snake! Insert dramatic kung fu fighting montage."

Dennis (guide monk): "Not so fast. I want to Push to control the Master's fate. The renegade is at least as good as the Master, and the renegade is fresh. The Master is losing the fight."

Dennis wins the vote.

Addie (Master): "Damn! Okay, the Master is weary, and gets thrown to the ground after a particularly brutal flurry. It looks like he might be finished. Then slowly, painfully, he gets back up and deliberately faces off against the renegade. He's knows he's staring death in the face, but he's going to go down fighting. He's thinking that the old blind monk was right and takes consolation from the fact that at least Wen escaped..."

Cat (Wen): "Yeah, Wen is watching all of this from the shadows with the other monk, and he can see his Master is in trouble. He can't just leave him. Wen's going back."

Dennis (guide monk): "And that answers the Question. End of Scene."

Addie (Master): "Hey, I want to clobber that guy! Don't we get to say how the fight turns out?"

Dennis (guide monk): "Nope. If we want to see more of this Event, someone needs to make another Scene."

Dictating Scenes

Instead of playing a Scene, the current player can choose to dictate what happens during the Scene. Dictating a Scene is useful when you want total control over what happens or when playing out the Scene would not be interesting. Other players cannot affect dictated Scenes.

Skip all the rules for making and playing Scenes and do the following instead:

1) State the Question

2) Decide where to put the Scene in history & review what we already know

3) Narrate what happens to answer that Question

You can include any characters you like and narrate whatever you want, but keep it short and to the point. When you're finished, follow the normal rules for ending a Scene.

EXAMPLE: MAKING A DICTATED SCENE

"I'm making a dictated Scene. The Question is 'what is the killer-machines' goal?' This Scene is in the Event when the robotic killing machines overrun the colony, before that Scene we played of Larsen escaping. The battle's over, and there are hunter-seekers roaming around rooting out survivors, but in the middle of the carnage we can see some more elaborate machines carefully harvesting tissue samples from the fallen colonists. It's clear they weren't really interested in destroying the unimportant colony. They're collecting genetic samples to analyze human physiology."

The player writes down the Question, the setting, and the answer on a Scene card, and then all the players discuss whether the Scene is Light or Dark.

Ending Scenes

A Scene ends when the players know the answer to the Question. If you think the Question has been answered, just say so. Don't get distracted by action in the Scene. You may be really curious to find out how something else in the Scene turns out, like whether the hero gets vengeance on the villain who murdered his father, but don't prolong the Scene to find out; just play another Scene later focused on that. If the Scene is going nowhere, the players can agree to call it moot and end without answering the Question (failure!).

After any Scene ends, whether it's played or dictated, do the following:

> Judge the Tone: All players discuss what happened and decide on the Scene's Tone. Was the outcome generally Light or Dark? Don't consider future consequences, just look at what happened during the Scene.
>
> If the Scene doesn't seem particularly Light or Dark, judge the Scene to be the opposite Tone of the surrounding Event–the Scene failed to live up to the expected Tone of the Event.

Write the answer at the bottom of the Scene card, along with a Light or Dark circle, then put the card beneath the Event it was in. Scene cards are stacked with the earliest on the top and the latest on the bottom. So if there are other Scenes in the Event, put this card beneath the Scene that comes before it, or on top of the Scene that comes after it.

Legacies

Legacies are common threads that may stretch through time and influence history. A Legacy can take many forms–an object, a person, a place, a blood line, an organization, or even a philosophical ideal.

> *The ideals of the founding fathers, a code of laws, a noble order of knights, an ancestral curse, or a sword fallen from the heavens–these are all Legacies.*

You make Legacies to identify things you think are interesting and want to keep in the spotlight. Legacies are explored during a special phase of play between one Focus and the next. Because you aren't restricted by a Focus during the Legacy phase, it is a broad opportunity to explore something that interests you. Just like anything in the history, a Legacy can also be brought into play or explored during normal play.

Choose a New Legacy

The player to the right of the Lens looks back over what happened during this Focus and picks something to be a Legacy. It has to be something that appeared in play this round, either for the first time or reappearing from earlier in the game. You are not making something new, just singling out something already in the history. Choose something you are interested in and want to explore more. It has to be something specific from the history, not a broad concept or idea.

> *'Betrayal' is not a valid Legacy because it's a generic concept. 'The Betrayal of the Sea Tribes' works because it's something specific that happened in the history.*

Write the Legacy on a card along with the name of the player. Fold the card in half and stand it up so it doesn't get mixed up with other history cards.

If you already have a Legacy, you can only make a new one if you remove your old one. There can only be as many Legacies as there are players. That thing still exists in the history; it just isn't a Legacy. If another player wants to keep your old Legacy, they can choose to immediately drop their own Legacy and replace it with the one being discarded. Repeat as needed. Having your name on a Legacy gives you no special authority except to decide whether to keep or replace that Legacy.

Explore a Legacy

The same player picks a Legacy and makes an Event or dictated Scene about it (not a Period or played Scene). It does not have to be the Legacy they just created. Since this is between Lenses, there is no required Focus, just the Legacy itself. When that is done the Legacy phase ends and the next player becomes the new Lens.

Style of Play: Getting in the Microscope Mindset

The history will not turn out the way you expected. Abandon your preconceptions. What other players add will surprise you, but what you add will probably surprise them too. That's good. The history you arrive at will be far more interesting than if you planned it out by committee and consensus.

No player owns anything in the history. Another player can take a beautiful metropolis you lovingly introduced and destroy it with nuclear fire, but they can't change what's already happened. Even if something is destroyed, it is never removed from play because you can always jump back in time and explore when it was still around. The past is never closed.

When it's your turn to add to the history, don't negotiate or discuss what you are making. Don't take a poll. It's your decision. You have absolute power. Likewise, do not ask a player to change something just because you don't like it. Outside Scenes, you have no power to veto or reject what other players create (unless their addition breaks the rules). Inside Scenes, you can Push you own ideas, but you can't change theirs.

Speak first, then write. The cards will help you remember your history, but what the other players hear and remember is more important than what you write down.

When someone else is making something and you don't have a clear picture or you don't understand how it fits into the history, ask questions. Ask for clarification. Everyone must have a clear picture of what is being added to the history so that they can build on it later.

Microscope in Play: Doom of the Gods

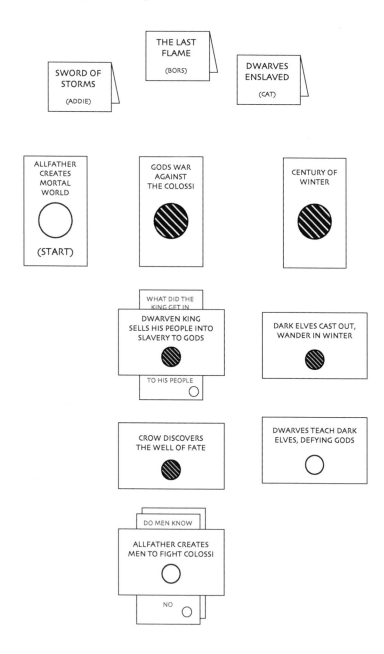

THE LAST
FLAME

(BORS)

SWORD OF
STORMS

(ADDIE)

DWARVES
ENSLAVED

(CAT)

ALLFATHER
CREATES
MORTAL
WORLD

(START)

GODS WAR
AGAINST
THE COLOSSI

CENTURY OF
WINTER

WHAT DID THE
KING GET IN

DWARVEN KING
SELLS HIS PEOPLE INTO
SLAVERY TO GODS

TO HIS PEOPLE

DARK ELVES CAST OUT,
WANDER IN WINTER

CROW DISCOVERS
THE WELL OF FATE

DWARVES TEACH DARK
ELVES, DEFYING GODS

DO MEN KNOW

ALLFATHER CREATES
MEN TO FIGHT COLOSSI

NO

PALETTE

YES
- GODS CAN BE KILLED
- ALL WORLDS PHYSICALLY CONNECTED
- INTELLIGENT SWORDS

NO
- RAISING THE DEAD
- MORTAL WIZARDS

FOCUS

1) ROMANCE OF GOORASH AND SVETKA

2) WELL OF FATE

3) DARK ELVES

HEROES OF THE SEVEN KINGS

FLOURISHING KINGDOMS OF MEN

DEATH OF THE GODS

(END)

WHAT DOES THE

DWARVEN OUTCAST VISITS WELL OF FATE

THE SECRET TO KILL THE GODS

GOORASH SAVES SVETKA FROM BLACK BEAST

WHAT DOWRY DOES SVETKA'S

MARRIAGE OF SVETKA INTERRUPTED

SWORD OF STORMS

WHY DID THE ALLFATHER

ALLFATHER HIDES LAST FLAME, REVEALS PLANS TO CROW

CARRY THEIR OWN FATE

GOORASH WINS SWORD OF STORMS

SVETKA MOURNS DEATH OF GOORASH

Ending the Game

Given that the game is all about delving deeper and deeper, it may not surprise you that Microscope has no defined ending. There are no victory conditions, no goal except to create something that interests you. Play for as long as you want, then stop.

If you're nearing your time to stop playing, it's good to agree before you start a Focus that it's going to be your last for the session. That way everyone has fair warning the game is going to end and can play towards a satisfying conclusion. Always end by playing the Legacy phase since it can provide a nice epilogue for the session.

Storing Your History

When you're done playing, you can keep your history intact by just stacking your cards in order. First, pick up the starting Period card, and then take the first Event beneath it along with its Scene cards and put them beneath the Period in the stack. Pick up each remaining Event and its Scenes in that Period. Then pick up the next Period card and repeat. So long as you go in order and always put the cards on the bottom of the stack, you'll have your entire history in chronological order when you're done.

When you want to play again, just lay out the cards, starting from the first Period on the top of the deck. Whenever the orientation of a card changes, you know it's a new Event or Period. Just make sure not to shuffle your cards.

Continuing Your History

Still fascinated with the history you played? You probably left the table with more ideas than you started with. You can easily return to a history and keep exploring it, session after session.

The one caveat is that you can't add new players to an existing game. Playing Microscope requires a strong understanding of what has already happened and a confidence in your creative authority. No matter how much you brief players who weren't in the history at the start, they may unintentionally contradict established facts (leading you to correct them, which is no fun for anyone) or they may feel unsure about what fits "your" history.

DISCUSSION & ADVICE

History Seeds

Need a nudge to get going? Try using one of these as the one-line summary of your history. Pick one that looks interesting or just choose randomly.

> *Long-separated branches of humanity stumble upon each other again in the depths of space*
>
> *Explorers settle a new land, displacing the native people*
>
> *Secret societies carefully steer the course of civilization*
>
> *Primitives leave their caves and found the first cities*
>
> *Superheroes protect society, undermining the rule of law*
>
> *A race of machines unearth their organic origins*
>
> *How the West was won (alternate history America)*
>
> *Gods play with heroes' fates until Doom takes them all*
>
> *The teachings of the Prophet are embraced by many, but bitterly rejected by others*
>
> *Technology brings humanity into a golden age*
>
> *The ancient Enemy spreads its dark hand across the land*
>
> *Battle of the Planets*
>
> *Renaissance: society shakes off the shackles of ignorance and embraces art and learning*
>
> *Colonists tame a new world, but are cut off from the old*
>
> *The health of the kingdom is bound to the life of the king*
>
> *Atlantis sinks and her secrets are lost with her*
>
> *Evolution of a species*
>
> *Captains of Industry: corporations dominate society*
>
> *A brilliant world-conqueror leaves behind a fractured and feuding empire*
>
> *Scattered refugees struggle to rebuild after the Apocalypse*
>
> *The last Magic passes from the world*

Don't worry if it doesn't look terribly interesting: a simple start is okay. Your history will blossom into something unique as you play. Even if you use the same seed again, you will wind up with a very different history each time.

Teaching Microscope

So you've read or played Microscope, and now you want to show other people how to play. You may be starting a game with your regular group, or you might be sitting down with total strangers at a con or a game meetup group.

This script will help you walk people through the game for the first time. It isn't a complete recap of the rules, just advice on how to explain them. It's presumed you already understand the rules. Read the italics sections out loud.

Teaching Step 1: Explain the Concept

First, read the "What Is Microscope?" section out loud. Instead of reading it all yourself, have the other players take turns. Then say:

> *"The author of the game says I should read this part to you because it's really important: All of us sitting at this table have equal creative power. At times we'll have different roles and authority, but we're all equal participants and authors.*
>
> *"It may sound like I'm running the game because I'm going to be explaining a lot about the rules, and I may interrupt and jump in to clarify how the game is played. But I don't have any more authority than anyone else when it comes to actually playing the game -- there's no GM.*
>
> *"Now that we know what the game's about, we're ready to get started."*

Teaching Step 2: Game Setup

Follow the steps in "Starting a New Game." You can read the first one or two paragraphs of each step out loud or just summarize, as you prefer.

Players new to Microscope may try to brainstorm too much detail about the history during the setup. Don't hesitate to jump in and tell players to save those ideas for later. Follow the steps rigorously.

> *"Microscope is a little like Poker: you want to keep your cool ideas close to your vest until you use them. If the rest of us know what you're going to do ahead of time, it's not as interesting."*

Teaching Step 3: Explain Play

"Now that setup is done, we're ready to start play. We already know more about our history than we did when we came up with the single sentence idea, and as we play we'll find out more and more.

"The basic structure of the game is that we keep going around the table adding to the history, making either a Period, an Event or a Scene. For each rotation there's going to be one player called the Lens, and that player is going to pick a particular Focus that everything we create has to relate to. So if the Focus is a city, each player is going to get to add something to the history that somehow relates to that city. It's a topic to keep us all on the same page.

"If you make a Period or Event, just describe what happens as though we're seeing it from a birds-eye view. You're in charge, and the rest of us are eagerly listening to hear what you have to say. If you make a Scene, we all pick characters and role-play to find out what really happened in that moment of history."

Teaching Step 4: Be the First Player

"I'll go first to show how it works, so I'll be the first Lens and I'll pick the first Focus for our history."

This is the critical bit. You're setting the example of how the game is played. If you do it right the first time, the game will go much better.

- Plan to make a Scene on your first turn. Playing a Scene right off the bat shows everyone where role-playing fits into the game. You'll have to plan backwards, deciding on a Scene before you make your Focus and Event.

- Build on something someone else came up with during setup to show how players build on each other's ideas. If someone else created an Event, make a Scene inside it. Otherwise make an Event in someone else's Period and make a Scene in it. Take their idea and run with it.

- Pick a Focus that is extremely concrete and specific: a person is best. Think about the Event you're going to build in to decide what will work. Don't worry if your Focus is pretty much a blank slate: what's interesting about it will emerge in play. Be very assertive describing obvious details (who this person is, their name, their position), so everyone can visualize the character and

60

they seem real. More details will come out in play, but start with a solid concept.

- If you're making an Event, describe it clearly, so players can visualize what happens. Include the outcome of whatever situation you create, and point out to the other players that you're doing this intentionally because we can see how Events end, not just how they start.

- Make something big happen. Create or destroy something, so it's clear to everyone that the current player has that power. Sack a city or narrate the existence of a big institution.

- Ask a very loaded Question even if you have no idea where it's going. Introduce a blatant contradiction: "why did this person do the thing they should not have done?" You want to get the other players thinking their own ideas about what the answer could be and where the Scene might go.

If anyone starts to discuss possible answers or character ideas, cut them off: tell them to save that for play. Being very strict about the process will lead to much better creative play. If the players understand when they are supposed to contribute, they'll be comfortable. If they don't, they'll be confused and uncertain.

Teaching Step 5: Playing the First Scene

During the Scene, remind the players that the goal is to answer the Question, nothing else. End the Scene as soon as it is answered, even if it's in the middle of exciting action. If the players balk, remind them that they are welcome to jump right back in and make another Scene to explore what happens next.

Demonstrate shaping the world by having your character perceive something. Introduce a secondary character if the situation allows. Don't introduce the Push rules unless it seems clear that someone disagrees with a description of the world–save that for a later Scene.

Teaching Step 6: Next Player

When your turn is done, remind the player on your left that they can make a Period, an Event, or a Scene (only one) and that what they create has to relate to the Focus you've set.

- If they describe something vague, ask for clarification. Be clear that you're not vetoing what they make–in fact, no one can veto their creation unless it breaks the rules–but it's important for all the players to be able to clearly visualize what happens in the history, so you can build on it later. Ask them to describe what we would see from a birds-eye view of the action.

- If they describe a starting situation but leave out what actually happens ("the invaders attack the city," but they don't describe who wins the fight), remind them that we would probably see the outcome.

Don't let them collaborate or take a poll, and don't let other players give them suggestions. It's their turn, no one else's. They get to make what they want to make.

Onward...

By now the ball should pretty much be rolling. You'll have to explain more details as you go, like how to Push or make Legacies, but you'll be over the starting hurdle.

The most important thing is to make it clear to the players how much authority each of them has to create (and destroy). If your game devolves into brainstorming or chatting about what might happen next, stop the game:

> "Here's another thing the author wants me to tell you: Part of the heart and soul of Microscope is to have each person contribute their own unique ideas, and then see how those ideas intertwine and grow on each other. If we plan things out as a group instead of contributing individually–if we collaborate rather than discover & experience–we'll lose that magic. The game will work, but it won't be nearly as interesting.

> "Resist the urge to coach, criticize, or make suggestions to other players. Helping explain the rules is great, but suggesting creative content is not. People may add things you don't like–that's okay. The game is designed to deal with that."

Strictly following the order of play should help.

Play Advice

These are some lessons we've learned from playing Microscope: things that work, things that don't, and ways to get the most out of your game.

What's a Good Idea for a History?

Here are a few things to check to be sure your starting idea will make a good Microscope game:

Lots of room: Microscope is more fun when you have a lot of time and space to explore. If you have a concept that spans a very short of period of time or encompasses a very small physical area (like a single city), then the players are more limited in what they can create. Lots of room, in both space and time, is also a creative safety valve. If a player isn't interested in what's being explored here and now, they can jump to somewhere else. In a smaller history you lose that freedom. If the entire history takes place in one city, anything that happens to that city impacts the entire history: there's no escaping it.

No preconceptions: If you have an idea in your head of how the history is supposed to turn out, you are going to be frustrated when people create things that don't match your preconceptions. It's a core premise of the game that the players have the power to make whatever they want, not to be stuck trying to follow someone else's vision.

A preconceived starting point is fine, so long as you are willing to let it grow unexpectedly. Steal an idea from a story, movie, or real world history, but don't expect it to turn out a particular way. Preconceptions about how the history is supposed to look are doomed, and trying to get the other players to adhere to the outcome you had in mind is doomed *and* bad form.

No one owns the history: This is another facet of "no preconceptions." Sometimes a player comes to the table with a particular idea for a history they want to try. That's great, but it doesn't give them any special authority in the game. They don't get to say "But wait, that's not how I imagined it would be!" There's a danger that, even if the person who came up with the idea does nothing, other players may still defer to that person's authority on what it's "supposed" to be like. People may not even consciously recognize they're doing it. It leads to hesitant, timid play with the other players second-guessing their ideas because they don't want to add something that doesn't fit the unspoken ideal. It's worth repeating: no one owns anything in the history. Once it's on the table, everybody has equal authority.

WHEN IN DOUBT:
Pick something simple, like "humanity settles the stars" or "the rise and fall of an empire." Don't worry if it seems boring or unoriginal: it will come to life as you play.

Beware Time Travel & Immortality

Microscope lets you jump around and explore the past or the future at will, which lets you move away from topics that don't interest you and focus on ones that do. Because of that, anything that collapses time undermines the game. Time travel is a perfect example: if the characters within the fiction can move backward and forward in time, the ability of the players to jump backward and forward is meaningless. The game becomes linear again.

Immortality has similar problems. It can work if lots of characters are immortal (like pantheons of gods), but if immortality is a special trait of just one or a few characters, they may hog the spotlight ("not Doctor Lazarus again!"). Another good rule of thumb is never to have character lives span more than one Period since that starts to weld adjacent Periods together. Once you're thinking about lifespan, you start to estimate precisely how many years must have passed, which locks things down.

Choosing Your Bookend Periods

Time continues before your start Period and after your end Period, but the boundaries you pick define what you agree to explore in play. You could take the same idea but change where you begin and end, and you would wind up with a completely different game. If you are making a post-apocalypse history, do you start after the dust is settled and survivors are scavenging for food, or do you include the days leading up to the boom, so you can play out how it happened? Either one works, but they will make very different histories.

Number of Players

Microscope works best with three or four players. You can play with more or fewer, but there are different impacts on the game.

Two players: Work great, except that each Focus is very short. The Lens goes, the other player gets one turn, and then the Lens wraps up (AA-B-AA, since the Lens can make two nested things). The Lens makes most of the history related to the Focus, and the other player only gets to make a relatively minor contribution before moving on.

To give the other player more input to the Focus, extend each Focus and go around a second time, but without the Lens getting to make a nested thing on the middle turn (AA-B-A-B-AA). Extending the Focus also improves continuity, because it keeps the history on the same topic for longer.

Five players or more: Not recommended. Each player has less chance to contribute. Scenes are also likely to be too crowded. If you do play with five, some players should volunteer to play background characters or Time more often (as described under making Scenes).

How Do I Make a Good Focus?

The Focus is a powerful tool to tune the pace of the game. Just like that little knob on the side of a real microscope, you can adjust the Focus to decide how closely you want to look at your history and how concentrated you want play to be. Stop and think about how the game is going:

- If play feels too dense or linear, a very broad Focus might help, like a place or institution that spans multiple Periods, because that lets players spread out and explore different parts of the history.

- If the history isn't engaging or it feels too remote or cerebral, a very tight Focus, like a person or a single incident, is a good way to build momentum and get people involved. Follow that up with Scenes with incriminating Questions (see "How Do I Make a Good Question?").

How tight does it need to be? That depends, but generally the tighter the Focus the better. Compare these ideas:

> *"Jake Howlett, veteran of the Seven Days War"*
> *"Jake Howlett's marriage"*
> *"How Jake met his wife"*
> *"The first thing Jake said to his wife"*

Even with an extremely tight Focus, the players still have a lot of latitude. "How Jake met his wife" is literally a very small moment in time, but you could still make a Scene on her deathbed thirty years later with the Question "Before she dies, does Jake's wife admit she knew he was an enemy deserter the moment she laid eyes on him?" It's decades later, but it still relates to the Focus because it's about how they met, and that's what matters. If the Focus is a particular soldier on the front lines of the war, the history you create may explore his death, his youth, or his memories of the war in old age, but all the players are still exploring different facets of the same tight idea.

An extremely broad Focus, like "Love", lets players roam all over the history. There's a constant theme, but each player could build on completely different times and places. That can be a nice change of pace, a "montage round" to let players explore, but usually a much tighter focus is better.

WHEN IN DOUBT:
Pick a person or a specific incident, and make it the Focus. It can be something or someone already in the game or something you make up on the spot. Don't worry if you don't know anything about the Focus or why it's interesting: that will solve itself pretty quickly.

How Do I Make a Good Question?

To be useful, a Question must do one thing: it must get all the players on the same page about what the Scene is about. The Question is the agenda for the Scene. It tells everyone what characters to pick and what they should be role-playing about.

The best Questions are extremely specific. Vague Questions are bad and lead to confusing or muddled Scenes. Open-ended Questions can work, but you will get much better Scenes out of very loaded or incriminating Questions.

There are generally two reasons you'll make a Scene:

- There's something specific you want to know about the history, so you have a particular Question in mind.

- You want to get the action rolling, do some role-playing, and immerse yourself in the setting.

When it comes to filling in the blanks of history, some of the best Questions are the obvious ones. Maybe there was a war, but no one ever said why it started. We've seen the tyrant but never saw how he seized power. Even if the answer isn't shocking, filling in those blanks gives all the players a firmer understanding of the history.

If you have an idea you want to explore, don't hesitate to stack the deck and make your Question more specific. A simple formula is to just add more conditions or "even though" twists to establish clear issues.

"How does the Alliance beat the invaders?" is a good starting point, but that's a very open-ended Scene.

"How does the Alliance beat the invaders even though they're outnumbered and outgunned?" is more specific. We have a better idea of the situation.

"Is the Alliance willing to sacrifice the colony on Sigma VII to beat the invaders even though the colonists will get slaughtered in the process?" is better still because it gives us a clear situation, an obvious dilemma.

If you just want to kick off some role-playing action, try asking a really personal question about a character, either someone already in the history or who you just made up. Think of something you would expect someone to do, then ask why they did or want to do the opposite.

A teacher should impart knowledge, so we ask "Why does the teacher lie to his students?"

A doctor should save lives, so we ask "Why does the doctor let his patient die?"

A captain should be protective of his ship and crew, so we ask "Why is the captain secretly planning on blowing up his ship with everyone on board?"

Those are incriminating, but pretty open: there could be a lot of answers. Again, make your Scenes better by adding more specifics:

"Why does the teacher lie to his students about who founded the colony?"

"Does the doctor save his patient even though he realizes he's the secret police torturer who killed the doctor's wife a decade ago?"

"Why is the captain secretly planning to blow up his ship with everyone on board in the middle of the Victory Day celebration of the very war he was decorated for fighting in?"

Those are all very personal Questions, but the answers can tell you a lot about the history, not just about the people in the Scenes. Maybe we find out the war was a horrible affair that left even the winners scarred. Maybe we find dark secrets about the colony's founders.

Avoid broad "what happens next?" Questions. If almost anything that happens can be considered a valid answer, it's a bad Question.

"What do the prisoners do after they escape?" could be answered by almost anything happening in the Scene. There's no clear agenda.

It may not immediately be clear why a Question is interesting. Don't be alarmed. Once you ask the Question, the other players get to jump in and run with it. They may have ideas you didn't even consider. So long as your Question gets everyone on the same page about the Scene, you're in good shape.

WHEN IN DOUBT:
Pick a character. Think of something you would expect them to do, then ask why they did or want to do the opposite.

Why does the miser give away all his wealth?
Why does the professor teach his students lies?
Why do the peasants decide to burn down their own village?

The character could be someone who's already in the history, but making someone up on the spot, someone no one at the table (including yourself) knows anything about, is a great way to get the ball rolling.

ADVICE

Implied Incidents: Keeping Track of What's Not on the Table

Periods and Events can include descriptions of things that sound like they would be an Event or Scene (respectively), but if no one actually makes them, they're not on the table. They're just implied.

> *A player makes an Event "a flying saucer lands at the capital." The Event can include all sorts of build-up and aftermath, but it's implied that at some moment a saucer actually lands. It sounds like an obvious Scene, but we could go through the whole game without making it.*

When you're making a Scene in an Event with an implied incident, make it clear when your Scene happens relative to that moment. Is it before the incident? After? Right when it is about to happen?

> *The "flying saucer lands" Event has no Scenes yet, so you make a Scene with the Question "is the government open-minded or afraid of the unknown?" and describe it as the President meeting with his advisors. But where does this Scene fall relative to the saucer landing? Are they meeting because the saucer has been sitting on the lawn for days and they need to decide what to do? Is it just a normal daily briefing and they're going to be surprised with the news, or is it entirely before the saucer arrives and we're not even going to hear about it in this Scene? They all work, but the other players have to know which you intend, so everyone is playing the same Scene.*

As you can see from the example, there are shades of gray: maybe the saucer hasn't arrived, but the authorities have picked it up on radar, so they know there's a UFO. Maybe they got reports of *something* invading their air space but still think it's a foreign aircraft, rather than aliens.

The same applies to making Events inside of Periods. If the Period is "the World-serpent awakens, boiling oceans and smashing lands," but no one has made an Event showing the monster waking up, then when you make any other Event in that Period you need to be clear whether it's before that creature appears (just another sunny day at the beach…), right as it happens, or decades later as the cities of the world have been smashed beyond recognition.

The players have a god's-eye view of history: they always know more about the future than the characters living through it. So in order to play those characters well, to really get their point of view, you need to understand exactly what they *don't* know. When you're looking at the whole scope of time, understanding a moment in history is as much about defining what is still unknown as it is about defining what is known.

Incomplete Ideas: Blind Man's Bluff

You can trip yourself up during Scenes by either having a complete idea, but only showing the other players a tiny hint and not telling them what you're really trying to make, or by making something that's intentionally incomplete because you want to let the other players fill in the blanks, but not making it clear that you intend them to join in.

The first usually happens when a player says something cryptic about something they have in mind, but the other players have no idea what it's supposed to mean. It's simple: if you don't tell the other players, they don't know, and it's not in the history.

> *"My guy pulls back his hood and looks at the newcomer carefully. 'Did They send you?'"* None of the other players know who 'They' are, or what the player is talking about. The players have nothing to work with, and it doesn't add much to the history, except uncertainty.

Even if you want to introduce something which you don't want the other characters to understand, it's better to have the players know what's going on so they can play along. A good trick is having your character think outloud.

> *"He says 'Did They send you?' and he's thinking about the news he got from his spies in the Scarlet Empire about the upstart necromancers from the East. He's afraid their power has reached this far."* Much better. Now everybody has something to work with.

If you are intentionally introducing something incomplete, make it clear to the other players what you're leaving out. When in doubt, just tell them what you're not specifying.

> *"Yeah, I'm saying that blips appear on the scanner, and they're closing fast, but I'm not saying what they are—my character can't tell. Anyone can jump in if they want."*

You may be tempted to describe your character's reaction without describing what you perceive in the hopes that the other players will seamlessly get it and follow along. This can lead to confusion and hesitation as the other players try to guess what you're hinting at. Don't be coy. Don't hold your breath and hope the other players can read your mind. You must describe what it is your character is perceiving and a reaction, not just one or the other.

> *Wrong: "The guard says 'Hey, did you feel that?'"* Other players don't know what you're reacting to.

> *Wrong: "The guard feels a faint tremor shake the ground."* Didn't describe a reaction.

Right: "The guard feels a faint tremor shake the ground. He says 'Hey, did you feel that?'" Describes both a perception and a reaction.

Right: "The guard feels a faint tremor shake the ground, but he doesn't think it's anything important." Describes both a perception and a reaction.

Wrong: "The guard feels a faint tremor shake the ground. It's a mole-man drilling machine boring to the surface!" (describes something the character isn't perceiving)

World-Building & Spawning a New Game

After a few games, the table can get pretty crowded with index cards. Perversely, the more you play, the more interesting your history becomes and the more you want to continue.

Sometimes you just become fascinated with a particular part of the history and want to really drill into it. One option is to spawn a new game by zooming in on one part of the history. You could take one Period, and then divide it into starting and ending Periods of a new history, or take two adjacent Periods and make them your new start and end. Take any Events in those Periods and place them accordingly.

You can also use Microscope to build settings for other game systems. Play one session, and you have a world that everyone at the table knows and likes. Make up some characters and go exploring.

AFTERWORD

How Microscope Works

Over the past two years, I've played Microscope with a wide variety of people, from old-schoolers to indie story gamers to people who had never even tried role-playing games before. In all those games, it's been fascinating to see how the unusual structure of the game–the freedom from chronological order combined with a vast scope of time and space–has surprising consequences on the way players interact at the table.

Great Power Without Great Responsibility

In a normal game, you play in chronological order so anything that happens influences what happens next. Events in the fiction have consequences that affect how we play the rest of the game. If the player before you nukes Atlantis, you have to continue play with the radioactive afterglow in the background whether you want to or not.

But in Microscope, even if a player does something that has a huge effect on what happens next in the fictional history, it doesn't necessarily influence what gets played next at the table. The next player has the freedom to jump somewhere else in time and space. There isn't even an assumption that you would automatically play out what happened next by default.

So you can explore that glowing crater that was Atlantis if you want, but you can also jump back and play in happier days or in the far future when it's been rebuilt from the ashes, or do something else completely unrelated. You may wish Atlantis didn't get nuked, but the fact that it did doesn't narrow your choices the way it would in a normal chronological game where cause-and-effect are foremost. And because the past is never closed, you can always go back to something in the history and explore it more if you want to. Nothing another player does can ever take that away.

It's a huge escape valve. Every player in Microscope has vast power over the fiction, but it works because, unlike a normal game, that creative power doesn't translate into controlling what the other players can or can't do. Once you remove chronological order and the direct cause-and-effect of sequential play, power over the fiction doesn't have the same relationship to power over play.

That freedom, the understanding that you are never trapped by what other players do, removes a lot of the need to say "no!" to things you aren't sure you like for fear that they'll inexorably take the game in a direction you don't want, like they could in a normal game.

Because players always have that out, they are also more comfortable playing along with ideas they might not like. They may not be thrilled by the idea of Atlantis getting nuked (at least not initially), but they know they won't be forced to deal with it for the whole game, so they're okay with playing some scenes in the glowing ruins. And because they're willing to give it a chance, they may discover the idea grows on them. They may even decide to build their own history to explore and expand an idea they would have normally rejected. That security allows them to be open-minded and experiment.

In Microscope, you also often already know how things are going to turn out. When you're exploring what happens in between, a player can freely introduce what looks like a huge threat or change without the other players having to wonder whether they should resist because they're concerned it might change the direction of the game. You already know how the fight ends, so you don't have to pull your punches. If we already know the *Icarus* returns from its maiden voyage, then you can have the shell-shocked XO take the bridge by force and threaten to blow up the ship. In a normal game, the players would be focusing on whether the ship goes boom. In Microscope, they know it's not going to happen (or that it absolutely does), so now they can focus on the characters and the meaning behind the action–on why, not what.

The Hotseat

Microscope gives players a lot of creative power, but it also *forces them* to use it. When it's your turn, you're in the hotseat. You have to come up with something to add to the history. No one else can make suggestions, and you can't ask for help.

This is an intentional design choice. I could just as easily have made the game the other way, with open discussion and brainstorming. There are two reasons why I didn't:

The first is that, by forcing each person to contribute their own ideas, without cross-checking or consensus building, you get a far more unique and unexpected result. Creation by committee inevitably moves towards established tropes and stereotypes. The odd and interesting bits get watered down. By comparison, I don't think I've played a single Microscope game where I wasn't surprised and fascinated by how the history developed.

The second is that, even with the best of intentions, when a group collaborates, social pressures mean that some people contribute more than others. Timid players may play game after game without ever making a major contribution, either because they're not confident their ideas will be liked or because other players are more dominant and their ideas are adopted instead. Gaming groups can fall into these patterns without realizing it.

The situation may not even be involuntary. Maybe the dominant players really do have consistently great ideas, so everyone is happy to run with them. Awesome. Maybe the timid players are more comfortable sitting in the backseat, not sticking their neck out and exposing themselves to other people's opinions of their ideas. Fine.

Rule systems that give players an *option* to control the fiction don't solve the problem because, if it's a choice, the same dynamics come into play: the dominant players exercise their mechanical authority confidently and the timid players are hesitant to use the rules to take control and create, again for fear that their ideas aren't winners.

Microscope eliminates that choice. If it's your turn, you can't back out. You have to make something, and the rest of us are going to sit here silently until you do.

Let's not harbor any illusions: the hotseat can be very uncomfortable. Painful even. But what I've seen after fifty games, and what I've heard from playtester after playtester after playtester, is that players who were normally quiet wallflowers surprised everyone with their contributions–even themselves. People who no one thought had ideas threw down amazing stuff. Some found it uncomfortable, but were rewarded when they fought through it. Others jumped right in because they'd been waiting to have a voice all along and now the structure finally made everyone else be quiet and listen to them.

The hotseat may burn at first, but it pays off.

The pressure to create is mitigated by the fact that you don't have to make something awe-inspiring. You can just take your turn and add something simple to the history. That lets players ease into their new power. But even the humblest additions to the history may prove fertile ground for other players, who build on it in ways the original player didn't expect. And when that player sees the ideas they thought were lame being embraced and expanded by the other players, it's an unexpected pat on the back. They're encouraged to build more. It's a positive feedback loop.

Independence & Interdependence

If the game was just players taking turns making stuff up by themselves, it wouldn't be very interesting and it wouldn't be much of a game. Instead, Microscope intertwines creative independence with interdependence. One feeds the other.

On the surface, you make history all by yourself: if it's your turn, you make whatever you want, and no one else has any say unless you play a Scene. But the rules intentionally only let a player make a single layer of history at a time (or two if you're the Lens), so you're forced to work with what's already on the table, building on what other players created and enticing them to explore and flesh out what you start.

Scene creation has a similar feedback loop. The player making the Scene picks the Question and creates the setting, but as each player picks their character or reveals their thought their choice influences what the next player thinks about the Scene. And that's all before role-playing even starts. It's no accident that the last player to make history is the first player to choose during Scene creation: it gives them the first opportunity to influence the Scene and introduce whatever continuity they might want to carry over from their own turn.

I talk a lot about how Microscope forbids collaboration or brainstorming, but that's not really true. What it does is require that collaboration happen through the medium of the game, rather than through open discussion and normal social rules. You're having a discussion. You're just doing it through the language and vocabulary of the game. When you describe your Period, you're telling the other players what you want in the history. When you explain why you think your Event is Light, you're showing them what you think about the fiction. They respond by making history of their own, using the same language. The entire game is a dialog, just a dialog with it's own rules.

Fruitful Mistakes

The freedom to go back and explore any part of the history radically changes another aspect of play: so-called mistakes.

In a normal game, if something strange happens during play–if someone plays a character in a way that other people don't get or introduces a side plot that no one wants to run with, there is a natural pressure to bury the inconsistent bits and move on. We overlook the hiccups, prune the lumps, and strive to embrace a unified, logical vision of the fiction. It's a smart strategy. Gaming is raw creative improv, so naturally it can't always be as flawless and focused as an edited novel: it's the nature of the medium. We accept this and hand wave when necessary. We have to in order to move towards a coherent fiction that everyone thinks makes sense–not even to make a good story, just to keep the universe consistent and believable. If no one thinks the fiction makes sense, it's exposed for what it is: subjective, arbitrary make-believe. We lose buy-in (suspension of disbelief in other mediums), so no one cares. If no one cares, play is pointless.

But in Microscope, you can always go back and take another look at the things that seemed strange. There's no way to ever seal something off and forbid exploration even if you wanted to. Sure, the Sheriff seemed a little out of his depth when we thought he was supposed to be this tough lawman. Everyone thought it was just flubbed role-playing and moved on. But any time during the game, whether it's the next Scene or a dozen sessions later, any player could go back and explore why that was: why what we thought was a "mistake" actually made sense. Maybe the Sheriff's past is a lie. Maybe he was badly shaken up by something that happened that morning. Maybe he's really the Sheriff's evil twin brother. Who knows? If we're curious and we go back and play, we'll find out.

So what seemed like a mistake or a misstep becomes a fruitful inspiration for exploring the history. Instead of a negative, critical feedback loop ("you messed up!"), it becomes a positive, constructive loop ("hmm, I wonder why that would be..."). One player drops the ball (they think), but instead of everyone rolling their eyes and glossing over it, another player takes that moment of dubious play and builds something meaningful and interesting out of it.

There is no gap, no inconsistency or question, we can't go back and make sense of. If we're curious, we can find out. If we don't care, we don't have to. That also means that, even if no one runs with your idea right now, you don't have to weep that it's never going to see the light of day. It can always come back later. Everything is still on the table.

Time Is Not So Confusing After All

When I first started pondering how I could turn Microscope the Idea into Microscope the Game, I didn't think it would be easy to play. The whole idea of a game where you could jump backward and forward in time, exploring inward instead of forward, keeping track of a horde of unrelated moments scattered across time and space... I just wasn't sure people would be able to do it without popping a blood vessel. I had serious doubts.

I experimented with some fairly esoteric ways to record and recall history (fear the cyclical time spiral!) and different ways to distinguish between types of history (like categorizing things by whether they changed the course of history or were personal, private moments).

The goal was always to design a structure that would make it easy for players to accomplish–and even enjoy–this fairly daunting task of building a history from the outside in. I wanted it to be, if not effortless, at least fun, not confusing.

For a year at least, when I sat people down at a table to teach them how to play, I went through a whole song-and-dance about how what we were going to do might be hard. "It can be challenging," I would say, "but don't worry, you can do it."

It took me a very long time, a surprisingly long time, to recognize that my expectations were completely wrong. People did not have a hard time keeping it all straight. They did not have a hard time starting off with big ideas and then zooming in to the details. Rather, it was the opposite: it seemed strangely natural despite the fact that it was different from any game they had played (assuming they had gamed before at all).

On one hand, I think this means the fairly straightforward Period-Event-Scene outline the game uses to map history is a good one (sorry, time spiral!). But, more importantly, I think it says something about how people actually think. We experience life linearly, moving forward in time, but we process and group our experiences into larger and larger blocks for easy storage and recall. When did you meet that person? You don't think: March 14th, 2009. You think: "That was after I graduated from college when I lived on the West side." We translate linear memories into hierarchical outlines all the time.

Outside-in, simpler-to-more-detailed, is also how we learn about new things all the time. Try explaining the electoral college, World War I, or some random movie you saw. I'll bet you start off with a grand summary before drilling down into the details. And even when you drill down, you don't jump straight to the nitty gritty ("Want to learn about World War I? Let me start by telling you about the first pilot to take out a zeppelin with a biplane..."). You lay out a succession of summaries of the entire picture, each more detailed than the last, until you finally get down to brass tacks. It happens every time someone tells you what happened: "Bob and Katie broke up!" Oh really? "Yeah, they were at a party Saturday night and got in a big fight, so she told him to shove off." What happened? "Well, first he showed up an hour late, then when they got there he was spending all his time talking to Alex..." Summary, expanded summary and then, eventually, details.

News, history, textbooks–it's all the same. It's how we educate ourselves about the world around us because it's an efficient way to learn. And just like Microscope, we're selective: we drill down and learn lots about topics that interest us, but in other cases we're happy knowing just enough to see the big picture.

Thanks

More than 150 people have playtested Microscope over the past two years. For everyone who gave their time to explore and experiment, I honestly can't thank you enough. You've made Microscope the game it is now.

Even when you love it, game design can be a long and sometimes arduous process. Without the help and insight of a lot of people, this game would never have gotten done:

Haskell, the ultimate Microscope playtester, for always giving me "that look" when I was tempted by very un-Microscopy rule changes. Mike for always having time to listen to one more tweak (no really, just one more!). My Mom, Carole Robbins, who pulled me through the homestretch and provided a much-needed pair of keen eyes.

Ping, who has played more games of Microscope and taught more people to play than anyone else. Without her, Microscope simply would not have happened.

And finally, my Dad, Michael Robbins, to whom this game is dedicated. He came up with finger-voting to solve my thorny democratic problem. But long before that, he was the very first person I explained Microscope to, back when it was still a half-formed kernel in my mind. He got it immediately.

...and thanks for playing

A game means nothing unless it's played. I've played in a lot of really fantastic Microscope games with a lot of different people, but I wanted to thank just a few who helped make my very favorites, the games that shaped Microscope's direction and proved to me it could work:

Ping and Haskell for countless excellent and formative games, from our Starcraft-analog to God Returns to Earth and many, many others (including half the games listed below).

Mike and Jem for the seminal Stellar Empire game. It was the very first Microscope game and still one of the best.

Tony and Paul for priceless hours of Xeno-Extermination. Always ban the sentient sun.

Eric, Kynnin and Gilbert for exploring The Godhead at Go Play NW 2010 and taking a bittersweet leap of faith in the mind of a dying scientist.

Pat and Robert for the war with Eurasia, the game that pretty much nailed the rules shut.

Playtesters

Players are listed by the first version they played. I know there are people who played but aren't listed here: my thanks to all you unsung heroes too.

Versions One & Two

Ching-Ping Lin, Jem Lewis, John Harper, Kevin Lewis, Mike Frost, Paul Riddle, Robert Haskell, Ryan Dunleavy, Tony Dowler, Trey Marshall

Version Three

Adam Drew, Adam Flynn, Alex La Hurreau, Amy Fox, Andy Stanford, Austin Smith, Benjamin Key, Bret Gillan, Brian Ballsun-Stanton, Britt Scharringhausen, Bruce Anderson, Christopher Pullen, Courtny Hopen, Dain Lybarger, Dan Eison, Dan Hertz, Daniel Goupil, Daniel Taylor, Deirdra Kiai, Dennis Taylor, Eli Zukowski, Ellen Panetto, Eric Borzello, Eric Raehn, Eshed Magali, Fabian Schindler, Gabriel Sorrel, Gavin Cummins, George Austin, Guy Srinivasan, Heather Constantine, Holly Lyne, Ian Dall, Ian Law, James Cosby, James Dobbs, Jan Laszczak, Jason Dettman, Jason Lorenzetti, Jeff Barnes, Jeffrey Kelly, Jeremiah Cunkle, Joe Iglesias, Joe Mottram, Jonathan Davis, Jorge Montesdeoca, Joshua Hitchins, Joshua Riley, Juliusz Doboszewski, Karina Graj, Kirsty Mottram, Kynnin Scott, Laura Owen, Malcolm Taylor, Marco Leclerc, Mark Townshend, Mathieu Bélanger, Matthew McComb, Megan Crozat, Megan Dobbs, Melissa "Mouse" Douglas, Michael Pevzner, Mikhail Bonch-Osmolovskiy, Monica Mann, Morgan Crooks, Morgan Rushing, Nicholas Marshall, Nicole Cunkle, Ola Samonek, Paul Montesdeoca, Peter Martin, Przemek Zańko, Rani Sharim, Riley Perryman, Robert Baker, Roger Carbol, Sam Atkinson, Sam Zeitlin, Samuel Lee, Shawn Wretham, Susan Kim, Tom Seaton, Tommi Enenkel, Villum Lassen

Go Play NW 2009: Daniel Wood, David Drake, Douglas Bartlett, Hans Otterson, Jackson Tegu, Jonathan Lemer, Julian Michels, Kelly O'Hara, Kingston Cassidy, Michael Decuir, Michael Petersen, Mike Sugarbaker, Philip LaRose, Ralph Mazza, Ronald Steinke, Ryan Forsythe, Suzi Soroczak

Versions Four & Five

Cameron Merrick, Cameron Parkin, Chadwick Ginther, Dale Horstman, Daniel Stoltenberg, Daniel Worthington, David Dunn, Erin Sara Beach-Garcia, Frank Krivak, Gilbert Podell-Blume, James Brown, Jeffrey Hosmer, Matthew MacHutchon, Max Reichlin, Meg Higgins, Mona Hinds, Nick Lundback, Patty Kirsch, Perry Grosshans, Rachel Brunner, Robin Ghetti, Sam Kaviar, Sean Leventhal, Sean Li, Seth Richardson, Sohum Banerjea

Story Games Seattle: Brian Williams, Caroline Gibson, Cy Myers, Dave Fooden, Eric Logan, Jamie Fristrom, Jason Wodicka, Jered Danielson, John Aegard, Joseph, Josh Verburg-Sachs, Marc Hobbs, Martin, Mike Kimmel, Pat Kemp, Remi, Rob Jones, Robert Hennes, Shuo Meng, Susan Taylor, Sylvia Luxenburg Wodicka

GAME SETUP

1) Big Picture: Pick a concept for your history, no more than a single sentence.

2) Bookend History: Make start and end Periods.

3) Palette—Add or Ban Ingredients: Each player can add or ban one thing from the **Palette**. Repeat until a player doesn't want to add or ban anything; all players should be happy with the Palette.

   Group decisions are now over.

4) First Pass: Each player makes a Period or Event, in any order.

OVERVIEW OF PLAY

Decide who goes first. That player becomes the first **Lens.**

1) Declare the Focus: The Lens decides the current **Focus.**

2) Make History: Each player takes a turn and makes either a Period, Event or Scene. Start with the Lens and go around the table to the left. Lens is allowed to make two nested things (a Period with an Event inside it, or an Event with a Scene inside it).

3) Lens Finishes the Focus: After each player has taken a turn, the Lens gets to go again and Make History one more time, again making two nested things if desired.

After the Focus is finished, we examine **Legacies:**

4) Choose a Legacy: Player to the right of the current Lens picks something that appeared during this last Focus and makes it a Legacy.

5) Explore a Legacy: Same player creates an Event or Dictated Scene that relates to one of the Legacies.

6) New Lens: The player to the left of the Lens then becomes the new Lens and picks a new Focus (start again from step 1).

Before you start the next Focus, take a break. Talk about how the game is going, but don't discuss what you want to have happen later. Keep your ideas to yourself.

MAKING HISTORY

On your turn, make either a Period, Event or Scene:

Period: Place between two Periods. Describe the Period and say whether it is Light or Dark.

Event: Place inside a Period. Describe the Event and say whether it is Light or Dark.

Scene: Place inside an Event. Choose whether to play or dictate the Scene.

What you make must relate to the Focus set by the Lens. Do not contradict what's already been said. Do not use anything from the No column of the Palette.

The Lens is allowed to create two things on each of their turns, so long as one is inside the other (an Event and a Scene inside it, or a Period and an Event inside it).

STYLE OF PLAY

After setup, do not negotiate or discuss as a group (except to decide the Tone after a Scene). Do not ask for suggestions or give suggestions. Keep your ideas close to the vest.

Create clearly and boldly. When you're making history, you're in charge of creating reality. Pitch your vision. No one owns anything in the history. Create or destroy whatever you want.

Abandon your preconceptions. History will not turn out the way you expect. Think on your feet and work with what other players introduce.

PERIOD CARD

EVENT CARD

○

SCENE CARD

MAKING A PLAYED SCENE

1) State the Question

2) Set the Stage: What do we already know from the history? Where is the Scene physically taking place? What is going on?

3) Choose Characters: List banned and required characters (max 2 each). All players pick characters (↻). Choose a character that helps you answer the Question.

4) Reveal Thoughts (↻)

Steps marked ↻ go around the table to the right, opposite of the normal order, starting to the right of the player making the Scene.

PLAYING A SCENE

Always move towards answering the **Question** of the Scene.

♦ Roleplay what your character does and thinks. If someone tries to do something to your character, you describe the outcome.

♦ Shape the world by describing what your character perceives and how they react to it.

♦ Introduce and play secondary characters, as needed.

Don't say what someone else's character does or thinks.

PUSH: CREATIVE CONFLICT

If, while playing a Scene, someone describes something about the world outside their character and you have a different idea you like better, you can Push to substitute your idea for theirs.

You cannot Push to change a player's starting character, except to change something they perceive or to decide what happens to them.

1) Proposal

2) Additional Proposals

3) Vote

4) Determine the Winner

5) Play the Results

ENDING A SCENE

When the players know the answer to the Question, the Scene ends. Discuss what happened during the Scene to decide whether the Scene was Light or Dark.